Happy Birthday

Linda

With love from Mom

D1277727

Book of Roses

Alice Caron Lambert is a painter, floral decorator and expert in floral flavours. In her research she has been guided by the fundamental harmony between what nature has to offer, and her own taste for botany and poetry. She is particularly interested in cooking edible flowers, putting together more than 450 recipes using flowers from her own gardens. She established herself as the specialist in this field with the publication of *La Cuisine des Fleurs* (Cooking with Flowers; ACR, 1995) and *Délices de Fleurs* (Delicious Flowers; Samogy, 1998). She advises craft workers and international groups on how to make new ranges of foods.

The publishers thank the Archives Départementales du Val-de-Marne, at Créteil, for making their pictorial resources available to them.

Alice Caron Lambert

Book of Roses

Illustrations and Design: Cooky Debidour

Half-title page:
Pierre-Joseph
Redouté, *Rosa
centifolia
mutabilis*. Coll.
Arch. Dép. 94.

Title page:
Song *The
Bouquet of White
Roses*, words by
Louis Fonteille,
music by
Etienne Arnaud,
1865. Coll.
Arch. Dép. 94.

Right:
Attrib. Antoine-
François Callet,
*Marie-Thérèse-
Louise de Savoie,
Princesse de
Lamballe*. End
18th century.
Musée National
du Château et
de Trianon,
Versailles.

Contents

Introduction

The first roses probably appeared 35,000 years ago: fossilised leaves from rose trees were discovered in North America. Myths and legends about roses show that they featured in the arts of every period. In 500 BC, roses appeared on coins in Rhodes, and on cuneiform tablets in Ancient Mesopotamia. They may even have been engraved on coins around 3000 BC by the Tschudes, an Aryan people. Sir William Flinders Petrie, the English archaeologist, discovered dried roses plaited in a ring in the tombs of Hawara in Egypt; they had been picked in 170 BC. From wild roses to the marvellous creations and magnificent hybrids grown today, this flower has always interested mankind. It is part of our everyday life and it also occupies an important place in our celebrations, in the development of remedies and, of course, in our imagination.

The rose, the queen of flowers, reigns over our hearts. We even go so far as to eat them, as though, in doing so, we seek to claim for ourselves some element of the divine in their make-up.

Below:
Young woman seated among roses. Coll. Arch. Dép. 94.

Following pages:
Sandro Botticelli, *Venus and Three Putti* (detail). Musée du Louvre, Paris.

The Secret of the Rose

Like the lotus in Asia, the rose is the West's most symbolic flower. In Islam, in the Garden of the Soul, it is an object of contemplation. The red of its petals reminds us of blood spilled and the distressing intensity of human passions. White roses symbolise the purity of young girls and the virginity of madonnas. Between heaven and earth, above the primordial waters, the rose stands for regeneration, its name coming from the Latin *rosa*, meaning 'pinkish', 'rain'.

Greek Mythology

In Greek mythology, art and poetry, roses are part of many legends. These probably relate to the wild rose, Rosa canina, *as garden roses were only cultivated much later. According to Ovid, the rose was born in a drop of Adonis's blood. Other sources say that the blood was Aphrodite's.*

The Roses of the Temples of Athene and Aphrodite

In Ancient Greece, roses were dedicated to Aphrodite, the very beautiful goddess symbolising fertility, and to Athene, goddess of reason and wisdom. On Rhodes, the Island of Flowers, they held initiation rites. Roses were then white as the foam on the waves. The beautiful Adonis was loved by Aphrodite, and when he was mortally wounded, he saw the goddess running towards him. In her frantic haste, she scratched herself on the thorns of some rose bushes. The roses, dedicated to the young god, were stained red by the blood from her wounds. Thus was born the legend of the rose as the symbol of love that endures beyond death, can conquer it and even regenerate life.

Above right:
Aphrodite Kneeling in a Shell, terracotta figurine. Musée du Louvre, Paris.

Right:
Fragment of funerary (or votive) stela, said to be 'In Praise of Flowers' (probably Demeter and Kore), Archaic Greece. Musée du Louvre, Paris.

Red Roses of Venus–Aphrodite

Aphrodite was seen as the most seductive goddess, and is the symbol of love's irrepressible power. She leads our senses astray and kindles our passions. She is woman in all her splendour; like the red petals of

Previous page:
Auguste-Barthélémy Glaize, *The Blood of Venus* (detail), 19th century. Musée Fabre, Montpellier.

Right:
Fresco with Blue Bird and Rose (detail), Knossos, c. 1900 to 1700 BC.

Opposite below:
Gustave Moreau, *Jupiter and Semele: Hecate, Goddess of the Night* (detail), 19th century. Musée Gustave Moreau, Paris.

Right:
Jacques-Louis David, *The Sadness and Sorrow of Andromache over the Body of Hector, her Husband, the Trojan Leader Killed by Achilles* (detail). Musée du Louvre, Paris.

roses, the flower dedicated to her, her flame is fired by the instinctive pleasures of a happy disposition.

In the Palace of Minos

When literature tells us of bull running ceremonies driving young boys and girls into frenetic dances, the sweet pleasures of roses were never far from the arena.

The oldest painted roses appear on the *Fresco with Blue Bird*, discovered in 1900 by the British archaeologist Sir Arthur Evans during excavations at the palace of King Minos at Knossos, in the north of Crete. These five-petalled roses may have been the *Rosa sancta*, the *Rosa gallica* or the *Rosa canina*.

The Roses of Achilles

Homer describes the siege of the city of Troy in Book 23 of the *Iliad*. He tells us of the death of Hector, son of Priam (king of the city of Troy), who was killed by Achilles. The latter carried a shield decorated with roses, and sought to avenge the death of his friend Patrocles. Hector's body was consecrated with oil of roses, then embalmed by the goddess Aphrodite. In Ancient Greece, oil of roses was obtained by macerating rose petals – probably *Rosa gallica* – in olive, sesame or almond oil.

olas Gosse
Auguste
chon,
meric
ne
nted
grisaille:
*tis Giving
ns to
illes*.
sée du
uvre,
ris.

Roses in the Labyrinth

A rose with a delicate, wild flower, lit and brought to life by the Sun, was engraved in the clay, then in the stone of the Labyrinth of Rhodes; it can still be seen today. The shape of the rose illustrates the course followed by initiates during their ritual test. Inside its elliptical form, the rings between its rows of petals stand for the path leading to the centre, where the Minotaur waits. Roses remind us of the vital force of blood springing from the ground. Hecate, the goddess linked to the World of Shadows, wore roses plaited in a ring. Roses were already thought to protect those who set off on the Road to Darkness with no thought of returning.

From the Gardens of King Midas to the Garden of Adonis

In the gardens of King Midas of Phrygia, son of Gordius – who was exiled to the fertile valley in Macedonia today known as Vodena – rose trees grew spontaneously, each one bearing more than 60 highly fragrant flowers. Perhaps these were the *Rosa alba*, with its full double petals. Theophrastes, the Greek philosopher and botanist (c. 372–287 BC), described many rose tree species in Egypt, and how to grow them. He explained that in some famous gardens, like the Gardens of Adonis, magnificent rose trees were grown in silver pots.

A Flower Dedicated to the Gods

In Rome, as a result of Greek influence, the rose was hallowed and used in funeral rites. It was accorded a divine origin because of the protection it gave for all eternity. In the most ancient times, roses were cultivated in large numbers. They flowered several times, even in winter. Despite their being grown at home, some were also imported from Egypt, as vast amounts of flowers and petals were needed for a variety of uses.

Above right:
Gustave Moreau, *Cleopatra* (detail), end 19th century. Musée du Louvre, Paris.

Background:
Pilasters from the tomb of the Haterii, Rome (detail), reign of Augustus. Lateran Museum, Rome.

Right:
Charles-Joseph Natoire, *The Triumph of Bacchus*, 18th century. Musée du Louvre, Paris.

The Influence of Bacchus on Roses

When morals became relaxed, the rose was appointed the voluptuous flower of love. 'Roses reign everywhere when Bacchus is in full cry,' wrote Martial, the Latin satirical poet of the 1st century AD, almost in regret. When there were feasts, the guests, and the slaves serving at table wore a crown of roses around their heads and another around their necks, for roses had the power to calm drunkenness, to soothe the humours and prevent people from talking too much. In this way, the rose became associated with secrets. The dishes and goblets of fragrant wine were decorated with petals and flower stems. The guests feasted, and slept on beds of rose petals with strong, heady perfumes, almost stifling in the moist and dense warmth of the velvety petals. According

Sir Lawrence Alma-Tadema,
The Roses of Elagabalus.
Private Collection, Paris.

to Ovid, roses were offered to Venus on feast days to
celebrate the founding of Rome, and at the festivals of Hymen
and Flora. They decorated the shields of conquerors and the
prows of ships.

Roses for Extravaganzas

The Emperor Nero spent four million sesterces (about £200,000)
on decorations and rose petals for a banquet. He also scattered
petals over a beach at Baia, near Naples. Five hundred years
later, the Emperor Elagabalus (AD 204–222), gave an
extraordinary feast, locking his guests in to make them watch
the spectacle he had dreamt up. Amongst other extravaganzas,
he showered the place three times with roses. So many petals
were used that several people died of suffocation.

Rome in the Gardens of Conquered Lands

'The sweetness of the scents of
spring and the beauty of the
flowers were such that we
might have been in the
splendid groves of Paestum.
Whichever way I looked or
went, all the streets were
bright with roses plaited in
rings. Oh Nile! As your
winters are forced to yield to
the winters of Rome, send us
your harvests and accept our
roses.
This inhabitant of the banks of
the Nile, eager to pay court to
you, sends you, Caesar, some
winter roses, a present of a
novel kind.'

**Epigram addressed to Domitian
by Martial in AD 81, from
Memphis.**

The Pleasures of Ancient Paradises

To the west of the Fertile Crescent lies the Persian plateau, now modern Iran. Persia was a paradise for roses and all kinds of flowers. Miniatures from ancient times record the magnificence of Persian gardens.

The Mediterranean Garden

The plans of Persian gardens were inspired by the traditions of Ancient Egypt, where planting was organised around reservoirs of water drawn from the Nile. These traditions were more than 3,000 years old, and imposed a style used from eastern India to western parts of Europe, as far as Spain. This influence also extended to countries adopting the Muslim religion, and also to Ancient Italy, giving rise to the Mediterranean garden. This kind of garden featured high walls, large trees, planting in straight lines, regular layouts, and a pond or central fountain.

Persian Paradise

In Persia, roses flourished at the beginning of spring, even when all the other flowers had wilted. It is thought that China roses, which flower continually, were brought to Persia as a result of conquests and trading.

The kings of Persia who ruled before Cyrus the Great (550 BC) were legendary figures, said to have lived and reigned for several centuries. Xenophon, the Greek historian active four centuries before the Christian era, wrote of these kings' passion for designing their gardens, where they grew vegetables and edible fruits, and ornamental plants and flowers.

The Chinese Influence

This appeared in the 14th century, featuring skilfully decorated structures. Flowers were planted in kiosks and arbours. No statues were used to decorate these gardens, but birds with wonderful plumage fluttered in murmuring streams; peacocks came originally from the forests of Persia.

Opposite above:
Contemporary Iranian mosaic. Private Collection. The word 'paradise' comes from the Persian word *Paradesha*, meaning a walled garden. These paradise-gardens, where they grew roses beside ponds and fountains, were places for meditating, walking, resting and meeting others.

Opposite below:
Dreaming in the Garden, House of Iran.

Right:
Meeting of the Persian Prince Humay and the Chinese Princess Humayun in His Garden (detail), Persia, c. 1450. Musée des Arts Décoratifs, Paris.

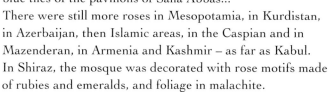

Redouté's Passion

Pierre-Joseph Redouté (1759–1840) painted more than 167 roses, most of which came from Malmaison. His paintings illustrate the famous work of Claude Antoine Thory, *Roses, Described and Classified According to Their Natural Order*, which appeared in 1817, four years after the death of Joséphine. Redouté contributed widely to establishing the legend of roses in terms of their sublime appearance, and that of an empress he loved very much.

Fantastic Oriental Roses

In Ancient times, the Arab botanists Ibn Amram, Abou Hanifah, Ibn el-Awam, Ibn el-Facel and Abou el-Khair wrote about rose growing, as did Ibn el-Beithar, the author of a 13th-century treatise on medicinal plants, describing 'the splendour of the rose bushes of Koum, a holy city. Tall rose trees in bloom, with their musky scents; ... were grown near the fountains of Tabriz, around the palace of Hasht Bihhisht; you walked on carpet-like surfaces, covered in rose petals, beneath cypresses from Eram; fresh roses showed their delicate colouring, blending with the blue tiles of the pavilions of Saha Abbas...'

There were still more roses in Mesopotamia, in Kurdistan, in Azerbaijan, then Islamic areas, in the Caspian and in Mazenderan, in Armenia and Kashmir – as far as Kabul. In Shiraz, the mosque was decorated with rose motifs made of rubies and emeralds, and foliage in malachite.

From an Island to the Garden of the Empress

Joséphine du Beauharnais, born in Martinique, was a lady of taste with a passion for exotic flowers and roses. With the help of skilled and famous botanists, she made her garden at Malmaison, in Rueil, near Paris, one of the most beautiful in France. Flower seeds were sent from the West Indies and the great botanical gardens of Europe, Central America and South America. Many specialists, stimulated by her enthusiasm, and

The 'Empress Joséphine' rose. Napoleon sent Joséphine seeds from the great botanical garden of the Schönbrunn palace, in Vienna. The empress took part in the development of rose trees, and was particularly interested in Gallica and Bourbon roses.

by her financial means, offered their advice. Two hundred and fifty species and varieties were planted, including *Rosa indica fragans* and the China rose.

The Gardeners and the Painter of Joséphine

In Joséphine's day, there were still no rose gardens: rose trees were planted in clumps, in the English style. For this new enterprise, Joséphine surrounded herself with eminent landscape specialists such as Charles François Brisseau de Mirbel, Aimé Bonpland and Etienne-Pierre Ventenat, and the famous painter and engraver Pierre-Joseph Redouté, whose publications include *Liliaceous Plants, The Gardens of Malmaison, Description of the Rare Plants Grown at Malmaison and Navarre* and *Roses, Described and Classified According to Their Natural Order*.

Opposite above:
Portrait of the Sultan Fahti Mehmed II, 1475. Topkapi Palace, Istanbul.

Opposite below:
Artist unknown, *Portrait of Pierre-Joseph Redouté*. Coll. Arch. Dép. 94.

Left:
Pierre-Paul Prud'hon, *Unfinished Portrait of the Empress Joséphine* (detail), c. 1814. Musée du Château de Malmaison. The painter had intended to put a rose in his model's raised hand. To the despair of the artist and the empress's entourage, Joséphine died at the age of 51, before the painting was finished.

Above: Edouard Manet, *Letter with Watercolours of Rosebuds*, 19th century. Musée du Louvre, Paris.

Right: Edward Coley Burne-Jones, *Princess Sabra, or the King's Daughter* (detail), 19th century. Musée d'Orsay, Paris.

'Rosy-fingered Dawn'

These famous words are by Homer, father of European poetry. Sappho, who lived on Lesbos in the 6th century BC, mentions in her farewell to the young woman she loved, 'the crown of violets

The Rose and Poetry

*T*he rose inspires intimate thoughts and writers. It does not illustrate them, it initiates them. It is the queen of the muses, and since Antiquity poets have invoked its mysterious powers and diverse symbolism.

and roses' that she gave her. A little later, Anacreon wrote in a well-known ode: 'The rose perfumes the song of the poet.' The rose became the flower of love: 'The rose loves love,' wrote Meleager, a Greek poet of the 2nd century BC, admired and imitated by Marot, Chénier, Musset, Louÿs and many others. This theme was adopted in Persia by great classical poets such as Hafez and, in particular, Sa'di, author of *Gulistan* (The Rose Garden), an erotic and mystical moral treatise.

Lyrical Airs

Pierre de Ronsard is certainly the greatest poet of the rose. The first verse of his sonnet on the death of Marie, his young muse, is universally familiar:

'As we see the rose on the branch in May...' In the romantic period, Théophile Gautier composed many sensual poems about roses for his *Emaux et Camées*. The rose he liked most was the Tea rose: 'The pink and diaphanous tissue of its flesh is of velvet,' he wrote.

Mystics of the Rose

'There is no reason for a rose,' said Angelus Silesius, a German mystic

Artist unknown, *Favourable Inspiration*. Coll. Arch. Dép. 94.

Below:
Sir Lawrence Alma-Tadema, *A Summer Offering* (detail), March 1911. Museum of Art, Provo (Utah).

of the 17th century. Rainer Maria Rilke, who died in 1926, wrote in his own epitaph, to be found on his tomb at Raron, in Switzerland: 'Rose, a pure contradiction, delight in not sleeping beneath so many eyelids.' According to William Butler Yeats, who in his youth had belonged to a group of theosophers, the rose is 'the West's flower of life'. 'Far-off, most secret, and inviolate Rose/Enfold me in my hour of hours.'

The Rose as a Woman

Like the English Pre-Raphaelites, the French Symbolists often put roses in their poems. Mallarmé: 'The rose is cruel, like a woman's flesh.' Verlaine: 'To kiss! a hollyhock in the garden of caresses...' Remy de Gourmont described it in his *Litanies of the Rose* as a 'hypocritical flower,

Below:
Artist unknown, *Small Girl Pulling a Cart with Roses*. Coll. Arch. Dép. 94.

Right:
Au Bon Marché, Riquet à la Houppe. Coll. Arch. Dép. 94. The rose is a symbol found in many tales and legends in all countries. It is frequently used as an ornament of beauty, the proof of a fête's magnificence, as in this illustration from *Riquet à la Houppe.*

flower of silence,' and Francis Jammes asked: 'You, O rose, mossy and fair, in your ears / My verses sing like murmuring bees.'

Alice and Her Friends in the Rose Garden
The rose is a magic symbol in such famous tales as *Sleeping Beauty* and *Beauty and the Beast.* In *Alice in*

Right:
Konrad
Dielitz, *Sleeping
Beauty*, 1879.
Slg. Archiv für
Kunst und
Geschichte,
Berlin.

Below:
Raphaële
Martin
Lambert,
The Little Prince.
Private
Collection.

'We are roses,' said the
roses.
'Ah!' said the Little
Prince.
And he felt very unhappy.
His flower had told him
it was the only one of its
kind in the world. And
here were five thousand
of them, all the same, in
just one garden.
'It would be very cross,'
he said to himself, 'if it saw
them... It would cough like
mad and pretend to die, to
escape being ridiculed, and
I would have to pretend to
look after it...'

Wonderland, by Lewis
Carroll, Alice finds the
gardeners in the Queen of
Hearts' garden painting
white roses red. Alice listens
in surprise as they tell her
that they had planted the
wrong type of rose trees.
When the Queen discovers
this subterfuge, she is
furious and orders: 'Off
with their heads!'

The Little Prince and His Rose

In Saint-Exupéry's story, the
Little Prince is suddenly
quiet and anxious at having
abandoned his rose, and
speaks to the geographer:
'My flower is short-lived,
and only has four thorns to
defend itself against the
world, and I've left it, all
alone, at home...'

The Little Prince in the Rose Garden

'Hello,' he said.
It was a rose garden.
'Hello,' said the roses.
The Little Prince looked at
them. They all looked just
like his flower.
'Who are you?' he asked
them, stupefied.

Mystical Roses of Christianity

The rose is the flower of all religions. Like the sun, the bird, the sea, a star, the cross or a ring, the rose has a symbolic value which acts on our imagination. The red, pink and white colours of its petals, its spiral form and its evocative scents have determined the symbols of the rose.

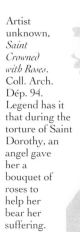

Artist unknown, *Saint Crowned with Roses*. Coll. Arch. Dép. 94. Legend has it that during the torture of Saint Dorothy, an angel gave her a bouquet of roses to help her bear her suffering.

The Madonna's Roses

'Who brought the rose and the cross together?' asks Goethe in *The Mysteries*. Roses are dedicated to Mary rather than Aphrodite, people preferring to ignore the latter in the early years of Christianity. White roses, representing purity, are often associated with the virgin martyrs, and the Virgin, the mother of Christ. Many tales relate extraordinary instances of roses appearing in response to the express wishes of the saint at the very moment of her execution. Roses bloom beneath the feet of the Virgin when she appears to men. When she goes up to Heaven, her tomb is filled with roses. Red roses symbolise Christ's blood spilt on the cross and his infinite love of mankind.

Roses and Rosaries

Rosaries originated in India, and consisted of 150 dried roses strung

together. The humble five-
petalled dog rose inspired
the symbolism of the
medieval Hermetics.
The so-called pentagonal
harmony can be seen at
the centre of Christ's cross,
in the rose windows of
Gothic churches and in
the rosary itself.

The Golden Rose
The first Golden Rose,
a jewel featuring a rose
in bloom with buds and
leaves, was blessed and

Opposite top:
Minuchio Jacobi da Sienna,
a Golden Rose from Basel Cathedral,
1330. Musée du
Moyen Age-Cluny, Paris.

Right:
Stefano da Verona, *The Madonna
of the Rose Bushes*, 14th century,
Castelvecchio Museum, Verona.

given to Duke Foulques d'Anjou by Pope Urban II in the Church of Saint-Martin-de-Tours. Alexander III gave one to Louis VII. In the Church of Saint-Jean-de-Malte in Aix-en-Provence, a fresco shows Raymond Béranger IV holding in his right hand a Golden Rose, the symbol of Christ's divinity. Until the end of the 19th century the Popes dedicated the Golden Roses given to princes of the Church with incense, Peruvian balm, musk and holy water.

Master's Apron (Rosicrucian), 19th century. Musée Crozotier, Le Puy-en-Velay. In addition to the rose, other Masonic symbols are featured: the mallet represents Intelligence, the triangle Durability, Light and Darkness, the cross the Axis of the World, and the open compass the Degree of Knowledge Achieved. The trowel is the attribute of the Freemason in his fifth journey of initiation.

Opposite top: The rose window of Notre-Dame de Paris.

Opposite bottom: Simon Vouet, *Virgin and Child with Rose*, 17th century. Musée des Beaux-Arts, Marseilles.

The Rosicrucian Brotherhood

In Christian iconography, the cross of Jesus bears five roses: one in the centre and the others at the end of each arm of the cross. These roses represent the Grail and the heavenly rose of Redemption. The emblem of the mystical Rosicrucian movement puts the rose in the centre of the cross, where the heart of Jesus lies, symbolising the blood He spilt for the redemption of mankind. This symbol also appears in the *Rosa candida* of Dante's *Divine Comedy*. In the *Roman de la Rose*, the rose becomes the symbol of the soul, and that of Christ.

Coll. Arch. Dép. 94

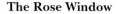

The Rose Window

The stained-glass west window of Notre-Dame de Paris has a complex form that combines stained glass interlaced with stone, and is one of the largest windows ever made. The wheel shape at the heart of the design features cycles and renewals. The wheel is a solar symbol, signifying the world in all its complexity, fullness and tragic brevity. Roses in the shape of a bowl also convey the same symbolism attached to the wheel. A seven-petalled rose represents the Days of Creation and the crucifixion wounds of Christ. In addition to these powerful associations, the rose symbolises the Resurrection and immortality. A rose without thorns is the flower of the Heavenly Garden where spring reigns eternal.

The Rose and the Alchemists

Treatises by alchemists are often entitled *Rosarium philosophorum*, 'rose gardens of the philiosophers'; white and red roses appear in several of their symbols. The seven-petalled rose represents the seven metals or the creation of the Great Work. 'The Rose of Arcanum XVII is that of the knights of the brotherhood, a flower placed on an acacia-wood cross. Faith will cease being blind, and sentimentality religious. Philosophical meditation will gratify souls anxious to believe in an intellectual way.'

German Christmas Carol of the 15th Century

A rose has sprung
from a root tender and frail
From Isiah we know
as the Ancients recall
A flower has bloomed
in the cold of winter
This rosebud borne
by the pure and only
Virgin,
As the prophet foretold
the beauty of eternal will
The divine Child is born
in the depth of night.

Roses as Historic Emblems

Many princes, religious orders, royal houses, political organisations and societies have taken the rose as their emblem or shield, using it as a sculptural, engraved or painted motif. Here we look at the important symbolic role played by this flower in various political events.

The Order of the Rose

Christine de Pisan, a famous 15th-century writer, objected strongly to the second part of the *Roman de la Rose*, credited to Jean de Meung, which she thought was a crude attack on women. She was helped by Jean Charlier, a great theologian and chancellor of the University of Paris and the Church of Notre-Dame in 1395. He set about writing a treatise against the work in question.

At that time, in January 1402, the Duke of Orléans organised a great feast dedicated to the rose, which Christine de Pisan attended. They decided to create the Order of the Rose, whose main object was to defend the honour of ladies, and all the men present became members. Christine de Pisan was encouraged enough to write *The Story of the Rose*, which portrayed the feast in the form of tableaux vivants. It was presented at the Hôtel d'Orléans on the day of Saint Valentine, the day of lovers.

The 'Lease' of Roses

By feudal right, the vassals (the dukes and peers) had to pay floral dues to the king in the form of a certain number

Right:
Heraldic crown interlaced with roses. Coll. Arch. Dép. 94.

Top:
Heraldic azure shield with a silver rose and gold buds. Coll. Arch. Dép. 94. On shields and coats of arms, the rose was usually depicted with five petals and a central bud; the latter had a different colour from the petals. The most famous shields are those of the Houses of York and Lancaster, and that of the Hocquarts, Marquises of Monfermeil in the 18th century.

The Oath of Knights
of the Order of
the Rose

**With good heart,
I take this oath and promise
And by the flower
proclaimed as the rose...
That forever
to keep my good name
I will protect
Ladies in all matters
Nor by me shall
any woman be defamed:
And for this I take
the Order of the Rose**

Tomb of Henry VII (detail), with
the roses of York and Lancaster
symbolising the Wars of the Roses.
Westminster Abbey, London.

Below:
Heraldic double shield on wood.
Coll. Arch. Dép. 94.

of bushels of rose petals, which was called 'the lease of roses'.
This most solemn ceremony was presided over by the king.
Members of Parliament and University
Councillors were crowned with roses
and carried a bouquet in their hands.
Parliament had its own floral officer,
called the 'Court Rosarian'.

The Wars of the Roses
At the end of the Hundred Years War, a
conflict concerning the right to the throne

First prize in the Rosati's literary competition, 1909. Coll. Arch. Dép. 94.

of Henry VI (of Lancaster) set the Houses of York and Lancaster against each other. This conflict unleashed a bloody and fratricidal war which lasted for thirty years. Each family had a rose for its emblem. The red rose of Lancaster was probably the *Rosa gallica* and the white rose of York the *Rosa alba*. Henry Tudor (a descendant of the Lancasters) took power in 1485 under the name of Henry VII. His marriage the same year to Elizabeth of York put an end to the Wars of the Roses. The red and white rose of the Tudors, *Rosa damascena*, became the emblem of the Tudor dynasty and thus of the royal house, and also represented the highest honours of the kingdom, such as the Order of the Garter and the Order of the Bath.

Top right:
The 'Peace rose', created on 29 April 1945 by Mme A. Meilland.

Right:
Drawing by Alexandre Lacauchie, engraved by Florenza, *Maximilien Robespierre*, Coll. Arch. Dép. 94.

Robespierre and Roses

Robespierre inspired the founding of the Rosati (an anagram of Artois), a sort of academic Masonic lodge, whose avowed aims were light-hearted knowledge and the praise of roses. Their meetings, events and concerts were held in rose gardens. This literary society was formed in Arras in 1778 by 14 friends of Robespierre, in memory of and as a homage to Chapelle, Jean de La Fontaine and Chaulieu. These young revolutionaries were not content just to hold feasts. They wanted everybody to be able to do as they did. In fact, their meetings were an opportunity to hold conversations that enabled them to plan the Revolution without being disturbed.

The Rosati disappeared during the 19th century. Not until 1892 did they reform and expand, first at Fontenay-aux-Roses, then in Arras and Boulogne, whose countryside is so romantic. Finally, throughout France, groups of artists, writers and scientists began to get together. These Rosati held literary competitions, performances of poetry and plays, exhibitions, conferences, baptisms of roses and scientific reviews.

Investiture of François Mitterrand at the Panthéon, 1981.

Jean-Baptiste Isabey, *Louis XVIII Crowning a Chaste Maiden*. Coll. Arch. Dép. 94. In 525, in the good old days of respectable and deserving girls, Saint Médard extolled the first chaste maiden at Salencey – his sister. Chaste maidens in the time of Chilpéric and King Clotaire I received a reward of 25 livres and a crown of roses.

Portrait Gallery

Until the end of the 17th century, the roses familiar to us were Rosa alba *and the wild roses of central and southern Europe: the Scotch or burnet rose, the eglantine, the damask rose, the French rose and* Rosa canina. Centifolia, *the cabbage or Provence rose, appeared at the beginning of that century, the creation of Dutch growers. The period is renowned for its travelling botanists who brought the first wild China roses back to Europe; these, unusually, flowered throughout the summer months. When crossed with French and damask roses, they produced many new perpetual-blooming varieties.*

The Origins of Roses

Wild roses are found throughout the Northern Hemisphere, but are unknown in the Southern Hemisphere. In Europe, more than 30 species are classed as wild roses. In North America, there are 25 indigenous species, but in China they have more than anywhere else.

Old Botanic Families

Wild roses and their cultivars are classified in groups. Many of these wild roses have been used as stock grafted onto others, producing a wide range of cultivated species.

• Caninae
Rosa canina
R. rubiginosa
R. pomifera
R. × alba

• Pimpinellifoliae
Rosa pimpinellifolia, the Scotch or burnet rose

• Carolinae
Rosa carolina
R. foliolosa
P. palustris (marsh rose)
R. virginiana (syn. *R. lucida*)
R. nitida

• Cinnamomeae
Rosa moyesii
R. pendulina

R. blanda
R. arkansana (a wild North American rose)
R. californica (California)

• Gallicanae
Rosa gallica
R. centifolia
R. × centifolia muscosa
R. damascena
R. × portlandica

• Botanical roses from China
Rosa holodonta
R. gigantea
R. foetida 'Persiana'
R. longicuspis (Himalaya)

• Synstylae
Rosa multiflora
R. wichuraiana
R. sempervirens
R. arvensis
R. helenae
R. brunonii
R. luciae

Below:
Pierre-Joseph Redouté, *Rosa gallica officinalis*. The Provins rose. Coll. Arch. Dép. 94.

Opposite:
Hokusai Katsushika, *Eglantine and Bird*, Japanese print. Musée des Arts Asiatiques Guimet, Paris.

Left:
Pierre-Joseph Redouté, *Rosa carolina corymbosa*. Cluster of Caroline roses. Coll. Arch. Dép. 94.

Previous pages:
Val Joanis Pertuis, garden in the Vaucluse.

Background:
Proposal for a genealogical tree of the rose. Coll. Arch. Dép. 94.

Above:
Pierre-Joseph Redouté, *Rosa canina (nutens)*. Dog rose with shiny leaves. Coll. Arch. Dép. 94.

The First Roses

Geologists and palaeontologists claim that roses appeared on Earth before mankind, and it is known that eglantines existed in the 12th century BC. The Greeks cultivated the *Rosa gallica*, a stock rose which created many modern roses, grafting it to produce, according to Herodotus, roses with 15 and even 20 petals.

Well-known Rose Families

The botanical species gallica, centifolia, moschata, alba, *Portland, the sparkling damask, etc., are still cultivated. They were and still are used for grafting and as a standard for the marvellous hybrid roses that we know today.*

Pierre-Joseph Redouté, *Rosa damascena variegata*. The 'York and Lancaster' rose. Coll. Arch. Dép. 94.

Rosa Gallica, the French Rose

This rose came from central and southern Europe, and was cultivated by the Greeks and Romans. It grows as an upright bush to about 1 metre (3 ft). Its elegant twigs carry large numbers of small spines. The flowers of an established bush have a strong scent and a diameter of 5 to 6 centimetres (2 to 3 inches); they are followed in the autumn by round red hips. This shrub is the parent of many old roses: the Provence and damask roses, etc. It has almost disappeared today in its original form (except for the Provins rose), but the species survives through its many cultivars: 'Belle de Crécy', 'Charles de Mills', 'Duc de Guiche', 'Duchesse d'Angoulême', 'Duchesse de Montebello', 'Leda', 'Gloire de France', 'Tuscany Superb', 'Empress Joséphine', 'Rosa Mundi', 'Hebes Lip',

Rosa × gallica 'Conditorum'.

'Celsiana', 'Complicata', 'Constance Spry', 'Scarlet Fire', 'Belle Isis', *Rosa gallica* var. *officinalis*, etc.

Rosa Moschata

This is the Autumn musk rose, originally from the Himalayas and cultivated in India. It was naturalised in

Rosa 'Felicia' (hybrid musk rose).

In France, *Rosa gallica* can still be found growing wild in the Massif Central, the Loire Valley, the South-East, in the foothills of the Alps, and in limestone and infertile areas.

Europe many years ago. It flowers profusely in clusters of white flowers with a musky scent.

These shrubs are fragile and do not like frost. They are still cultivated for their delicate perfume which is used for industrial purposes. Hybrids of *R. moschata* include: 'The Garland', 'Ballerina', 'Felicia', 'Robin Hood', etc.

Damask Rose

The damask rose was cultivated by the Persians and brought to Europe from the Crusades. The knight Robert de Brie introduced it in the gardens of his château in Champagne between 1254 and 1276. Damask roses with

a short flowering season are hybrids of *Rosa gallica* and *Rosa phoenicia*, the botanical rose. The bushes are supple and graceful, the leaves are long and pointed, and their lovely bright-pink flowers are very fragrant. The Autumn

The Queen of Princesses and Magicians in Ancient Egypt

Beneath a fine dust accumulated over time, and half-buried in the sand, the crowns of dried roses seemed to have been sleeping for eternity, like the Egyptian mummies buried there.

Sir William Flinders Petrie (1853–1942) uncovered the remains of rose trees during his excavations in the tombs at Hawara in Egypt. They were probably the *Rosa × richardii*, formerly known as the *Rosa sancta*, a cross between *Rosa gallica* and *Rosa phoenicia*, the ancient damask rose. These precious plant remains are preserved at Kew Gardens, in London.

Damask rose produced the perpetual-blooming Portland roses: 'Celsiana', 'St Nicholas', 'York and Lancaster', 'Quatre Saisons', 'Madame Hardy', 'Marie Louise', 'Le Ville de Bruxelles', 'Oeillet Parfait', 'Omar Khayyám', etc.

Rosa alba 'Cuisse de Nymphe'. The 'Dumont de Corset' rose (1802). Musée du Château de Malmaison.

Rosa Alba

This rose with white flowers was introduced to France and Great Britain by the Romans, and was widely used in pharmaceutical remedies in the Middle Ages. It was a hybrid between the eglantine (*Rosa canina*) and the damask rose. This precious group represents the oldest roses. The flowers are white or pink, delicate and superbly refined. Some *Rosa alba* are: *Rosa × alba* 'Semiplena', 'Félicité Parmentier', 'Cuisse de Nymphe', 'Madame Plantier', 'Madame Legras de Saint-Germain', 'Gloire de Guilan' and 'Queen of Denmark'.

Rosa Centifolia
Cabbage or Provence Rose

Also known as the 'painter's rose', this was introduced at the beginning of the 17th century by Dutch growers. It was a cross between the damask rose and *Rosa alba*. This is a large shrub with large, long and broadly toothed leaves, and fine spines on the branches. The flowers are heavy, fragrant and have many petals (hence the name 'cabbage rose'). These very popular roses appear in many paintings by Dutch and Flemish artists.

Rosa centifolia cristata. The 'Chapeau de Napoléon' rose. Musée du Château de Malmaison.

'Henri Martin' roses.

The *centifolia* include: 'La Noblesse', 'Tour de Malakoff', 'Chapeau de Napoléon', 'Fantin Latour', 'The Bishop', 'Unique Blanche', 'Rose des Peintres', etc.

Cabbage or Provence Moss Rose

This species develops sepals like moss. This 'moss' refers to the flower's glandular mossy calyx, which is much larger than that of other roses and almost covers the bud, giving the flowers a special charm.

Rosa centifolia muscosa.
The 'Feu Amoureux' rose.

The bush stands fairly upright, more so than the other *centifolia*. The flowers have a strong perfume, like their ancestors: 'Blanche Moreau', 'Capitaine Basroger', 'Captaine John Ingram', 'Comtesse de Murinais', 'James Mitchell', 'Mousseline', 'Jeanne de Montfort', 'Duchesse de Verneuil', 'Général Kléber', 'Gloire des Mousseux', 'Henri Martin', 'Goethe', 'Madame de la Roche-Lambert', etc.

Portland Rose
This comes from the English peninsula of Portland, and was introduced in France for Joséphine's collection at Malmaison, despite the English blockade of French ports. It was called 'Duchess of Portland' in honour of the woman who, in 1800, acquired a rose in Italy called *Rosa paestana* or 'Scarlet Four Seasons', which was the parent of the Portland rose. The latter is probably the result of a cross between a French rose and an Autumn Damask rose. There may also be a relationship with a China rose. A perpetual-blooming hybrid 1.2 metres high (4 ft), whose old-fashioned-looking flowers have many strong

Pierre-Joseph Redouté, *Rosa damascena coccinea*, a Portland rose. Coll. Arch. Dép. 94.

The 'Comte de Chambord' rose, created in 1862 by Robert Moreau, Portland.

fuchsia-red petals; they are highly perfumed, with a fairly rigid stance. In 1848, there were more than 80 cultivated varieties, created by English and French growers. There are few today, but they are superb: 'Comte de Chambord', 'Duchesse de Rohan', 'Jacques Cartier', 'Yolande d'Aragon' and 'Delambre'.

Pierre-Joseph Redouté, *Rosa noisettiana* Philippe de Noisette rose. Coll. Arch. Dép. 94.

we know today, such as 'Desprez à Fleurs Jaunes'. These vigorous climbers include: 'Aimée Vibert', 'Félicité et Perpétué', 'Céline Forestier', 'Maréchal Niel', 'Madame Alfred Carrière', 'Crépuscule', 'Boule de Neige', etc.

Tea Rose

These roses are the result of a cross between the China roses 'Hume's Blush Tea-scented China' and 'Park's Yellow Tea-scented China' with Bourbon and Noisette roses. The first tea rose was grown by an Englishman, Adams, in 1835. These are beautiful shrubs. The flowers have

Pierre-Joseph Redouté, *Rosa* 'Fragrance' (*indica*) – fragrant rose (from the Indies) – 'Hume's Blush China'. Coll. Arch. Dép. 94.

Noisette Rose

This rose was created by Philippe Noisette in 1802 by crossing a China rose, 'Parson's Pink China' (now called 'Old Blush') with a *Rosa moschata*. Philippe Noisette grew seedlings in South Carolina, and cuttings were sent to France to produce the 'Blush Noisette'. This, crossed with yellow-flowering tea roses, produced the typical Noisette roses that

'Félicité et Perpétue' roses.

various shapes and colours. Their pleasant perfume is characteristic, but fairly remote from the scent of tea. They flower perpetually throughout summer. They are sensitive to the cold, and in cold regions the hardy, fragrant, climbing tea roses do much better. Some lovely tea roses are: 'Chicago Peace', 'Duke of Windsor', 'Eden Rose', 'Miss France', 'Prima

Ballerina'. In 1978, Meilland created 'Galia', a bush rose with orangey-red flowers.

Bourbon Rose

The farmers of Bourbon Island (the old name for Reunion Island) used to plant hedges made of 'Old Blush' and Autumn Damask roses. A natural hybrid grew there, and was cultivated under the name

Bourbon rose 'Mme Pierre Oger'.

'Rose Edward'. Seeds from this rose were sent to King Louis-Philippe's gardener, and he produced the rose known as 'Bourbon Island Rose'. Bourbon roses were introduced in France in 1823, and in England in 1825. They are vigorous and almost all bloom perpetually. They have helped the creation of modern roses by preserving the characteristically large flowers and strong scents distinctive of old-fashioned roses, and the continuous flowering of the hybrid teas. They include: 'Souvenir de la Malmaison', 'Zéphirine Drouhin', 'Victor Emmanuel', 'La Reine Victoria', 'Madame Pierre Oger', etc.

Rosa × borboniana. The 'Boule de Neige' rose.

The Language of Roses

Pink rose: beauty
Provence rose: pleasure
Capuchin rose: innocence and frankness
Provins rose: patriotism
Bengal rose: strange beauty
Yellow rose: conjugal love
Moss rose: voluptuous ecstasy
Musk rose: lack of naturalness
Pompon rose: naïve grace
White rosebud: too young to love

Chinese Ancestors

In China, there are more than a 100 varieties of wild roses. The China roses shown here are ancient ones, brought to Europe from the 17th century onwards, and used as stock to modify our varieties when crossed with existing European species.

Rosa banksiae, Japanese print. Coll. Arch. Dép. 94.

An Enigmatic Perfume

Flowering rose bushes, imported from China, lay next to cases filled with tea during their long ocean voyage to the West, and perhaps were impregnated with the delicate scents of these freshly dried teas. The mystery remains unsolved, but the origins of these rose plants gave them a characteristic scent, even though it has little in common with that of tea.

'Old Blush'
(formerly 'Parson's Pink China')
This China rose was introduced to Sweden in 1752 and the United States around 1800. As a stock plant, it was crossed with Noisette roses, and may be a

Fò dog, Chinese ceramic. Co[ll.] Arch. Dép. [

parent of the Bourbon roses. It blooms perpetually, is 2 m (6 ft) high, with pink flowers and a scent of apple blossom.

'Slater's Crimson China'
Rosa indica 'Bengal'
A China rose introduced to Great Britain in 1792. It is a parent of the Portland and a grandparent of the perpetual-blooming hybrids. Flowers continuously.
'Bengal Red', 'Cécile Brunner Climbing', 'Bloomfield Abundance', 'Irene Watts', etc.

Rosa Bracteata
The Macartney rose
A China rose introduced to Great Britain in 1793.

Rosa banksiae lutea.

A persistent climber, 2.5 m (8 ft) high; single flowers with yellow stamens. Flowers from July to autumn; fragrant. Ancestor of 'Mermaid'.

Background:
Rosa banksiae,
Japanese print.
Coll. Arch.
Dép. 94.

Rosa laevigata. Coll. Arch. Dép. 94.

'Hume's Blush Tea-scented China

A China rose from Canton, introduced to France in 1810 by the British Admiralty for Joséphine de Beauharnais (despite their blockade of French ports). Perpetual; 1.5 m (5 ft) high; elegant white, fragrant flowers. Considered to be a tea rose.

'Parks' Yellow Tea-scented China'

A stock China rose, introduced in 1824. Close to the wild tea rose. It has been suggested that this rose is the result of a cross between *Rosa gigantea* and a China rose. Ancestor of the hybrid tea roses. Perpetual; 2 m (6 ft) high; yellow flowers; flowers in May. The leaves have a scent of tea.

Rosa Gigantea

(formerly *Rosa odorata* var. *gigantea*)
A rose discovered in Burma in 1882. Main parent of the modern hybrid tea roses; 2m (6 ft) high; single, pure-white flowers.

Things People Say

She's as fresh as a rose.
It's not all a bed
of roses.
Take time to smell the
roses along the way.
A rose between
two thorns.
It was roses,
roses all the way.
A rose by any other name
would smell as sweet.
Seeing things through
rose-coloured spectacles.

Rosa chinensis
'Mademoiselle
Cécile Brunner'.

Rosa Banksiae Var. Normalis

A wild rose, now cultivated as the Banksian rose. Can have double white flowers and double yellow flowers with a scent of violet; tall climber; 5 m (16 ft) high.

Modern Roses from Around the World

Today there are more than a 1000 varieties of roses. From all the great wealth of different rose species and their hybrids, we can think of modern roses as being the result of crosses between varieties obtained since the beginning of the 20th century.

Growing Delbard roses at Hyères.

Two Main Groups
– Hybrid tea roses. This is a large group, and the most popular.
– The *floribundas*. These were created recently, after crossing with *polyantha* roses. Their flowers are borne in small clusters, which makes them particularly recognisable. The stems, which bear several flowers, are derived from *Rosa multiflora*, parent of the *polyantha* roses. Their origins are very complex and defy classification.

The Advent of Modern Roses
Modern roses are the result of numerous crossings aimed at improving health, vigour, size and flowering period ... often to the detriment of the scents of the parent roses. The colours of hybrids now include deep whites, crisp yellows and oranges, bicolours, pink-mauve, and almost blue roses such as 'Charles de Gaulle'.

The First Rose Bushes with Yellow Flowers
In 1907 in Copenhagen, Dines Poulson created the first rose bush to be grown at his father's nursery. This was 'Rödhätte', a cross between a *polyantha* and a hybrid tea rose, and it was the start of a new group of hardy and

Pernille and Mogens N. Olsen
in one of their greenhouses.

rose, a hybrid tea with red flowers, and also a group of 'Kent' ground-cover roses. 'Chinatown': *floribunda*, 'Columbine' × 'Cläre Grammerstorf' with perpetual, fragrant flowers. In 1937, Meilland created 'Golden State'.

Tea Roses with the Perfumes of Asia

In 1901, Benjamin Cant, a gardener from Colchester,

vigorous roses. Svend Poulson, his brother, went on to create 'Kirsten Poulson' and 'Else Poulson' in 1924. These *floribundas* included the first rose with yellow flowers. Niels Dines, his son, continued his research and in 1963 created 'Chinatown', a *floribunda* with fragrant yellow flowers. Pernille, Niels's daughter, and her husband produced the famous 'Ingrid Bergman'

Svend Poulsen.

The First to Make a Modern Graft

There is no need to go back to the Greeks to find out the secret.

The credit goes to Dubois, Joséphine's gardener at Malmaison. He loved both roses and Joséphine, and his two passions gave him the brilliant idea, the sublime act that paved the way for modern roses. His words have been preserved: 'One day, the man who wants to declare his passion to the one he adores will have a choice of a hundred different roses, perhaps more... Alas, I shall not see that day...'

created the very well-known tea rose 'Mrs B.R. Cant'.
• Recent creations from the Cants of Colchester nurseries are 'Just Joey' and 'Alpine Sunset'.
• 'Lady Rachel': *floribunda*, 'English Miss' × 'Margaret Merril', introduced in 1990.
• 'Alpine Sunset': hybrid tea rose, 'Dr A.J. Verhage' × 'Grandpa Dickson',

Bush of 'Centenaire de Lourdes Rouge'® roses *delfloro* Delbard.

Bouquets for a Tea Cermony

William A. Warriner, a hybrid specialist, created many specimens by crossing *floribundas* and hybrid tea roses: they bear many flowers in clusters and pretty colours such as pure white and bright red, shaded with gentle variations of pink and yellow. Among the many varieties are: 'Simplicity', *floribunda*; 'Pristine', a hybrid tea, etc.

Truffaut has created 'Bordure Vive' and 'Bordure Vermilion', small, very hardy roses with many bright-red flowers.

'Centenaire de Lourdes' is a very profusely flowering *floribunda* obtained by

Delbard's 'Queen Elizabeth' rose.

Delbard-Chabert in France in 1958.

It flowers perpetually, and has a light fragrance.

Fire Roses

These hybrids of tea roses and *floribundas* have flowers with colours of yellow, yellow shaded with orange, and highlights of gold or copper. Albert Norman, president of the National Rose Society in Great Britain, and the Harkness nursery marketed 'Ena Harkness' and 'Frensham' in 1946. Jack Harkness created 'Merlin', 'Sir Lancelot' and 'King Arthur' in 1967. In France in 1992, the Meilland-Richardier company created 'Marco Polo', a rose with perpetual, good-shaped flowers in deep yellow with a peppery fragrance. 'Antony Meilland', a good *floribunda*, was introduced in 1990: the flowers are an intense yellow, but the fragrance is slight. Their most popular rose should also be mentioned: 'Madame A. Meilland', created in 1935; it is 1.2 m (4 ft) high, with flowers varying from pink to yellow, then red, according to the nature of the soil, the weather and the season. When it was introduced to the United States at the end of the Second World War, it was given the name 'Peace'. 'Tequila Sunrise' is a vigorous *floribunda* with richly coloured flowers, grown by Dickson in Northern Ireland.

Top right:
Old-fashioned roses. Little Malvern Court.

Below:
'Constance Spry' roses (Austin, 1961).

Perpetual Hybrids, Roses for All Seasons

George Dickson, the son of a Scotsman who moved to Northern Ireland, created perpetual hybrids and tea roses. 'Mrs W.J. Grant', a cross between 'La France' and 'Lady Mary Fitzwilliam' (*floribunda*), is the parent of many hybrid tea roses. Other varieties with red flowers followed, such as 'George Dickson' (1912). In 1919, Guillot fils created 'Comtesse de Cassagne', which produces large round fragrant roses in creamy white with highlights of ivory mixed with coppery tones.

English Roses

These are the result of a cross between old-fashioned roses and modern hybrid teas or *floribundas*. They were first created by the English grower David Austin. The first English roses appeared in the 1960s, at a time when old-fashioned roses were disappearing in favour of hybrid teas. The most famous is 'Constance Spry', with its scented, refined and beautiful bright-pink flowers which recall old-fashioned roses. It is a cross between the *floribunda* 'Dainty Maid' and the French rose 'Belle Isis'.

'Evelyn' is a large impressive rose with bronze pink-white flowers in the shape of a bowl, and superbly scented.

'Charles Austin' is the most popular. Its yellow sport (hybrid), 'Yellow Charles Austin', was introduced in 1981.

In Germany, Kordes Söhne introduced the pretty 'Snow Fairy' in 1958: this is an elegant *floribunda* with lovely white flowers and a light scent.

In 1977, Delbard-Chabert produced 'Grand Siècle', a very elegant hybrid tea rose. This perpetual-flowering shrub has lightly scented, pale-pink flowers tending towards white.

'Iceberg' and 'Fée des Neiges' roses.

Hardy Roses

In Germany, Wilhelm Kordes is one of the greatest rose growers of our time. He has crossed botanical roses with hybrid tea roses and obtained 'Frühlingsgold' (1937) and 'Frühlingsmorgen' (1941), which have *Rosa pimpinellifolia* as a parent; 'Fritz Nobis', a large shrub grown in many gardens; robust *floribundas* with yellow flowers; 'Fée des Neiges', 'Iceberg' and 'Schneewittchen', which have white flowers and a light scent; 'Lilli Marlène', a very profuse *floribunda* with crimson flowers for planting in the border – although it is rather sensitive to powdery mildew. 'Ingrid Bergman' is a marvellous hybrid tea with dark-red flowers and a light scent. Usually planted in clumps, it was created and distributed by Poulsen in Denmark in 1984.

Elegant Roses, the First *Polyanthas*

In Germany, Mathias Tantau produced the first *polyanthas* in 1918: 'Cerise Bouquet', a hybrid of *Rosa multibracteata* (about 1938); 'Floradora', the parent of 'Queen Elizabeth', in 1944; 'Blue Moon', a hybrid tea rose with an excellent scent, the best of the blue roses group; 'Whisky Mac' and 'Polar Star', with white flowers.

Rosa pimpinellifolia 'Frühlingsgold'.

'Intrigue', *floribunda* ('White Masterpiece' × 'Heirloom'), which flowers continuously and has a lovely scent, was introduced by Warriner in 1984.

In 1981, Meilland introduced 'Rustica', a pretty *floribunda* with cream flowers, which looks well as a standard rose.

In 1841, Laffay, a rose grower from Auteuil, created 'Néron', a French rose. This upright shrub bears superb, pleasantly scented single flowers in lilac pink flecks with a paler heart. It can be found in the rose garden at L'Haÿ-les-Roses.

In Belgium, Louis Parmentier introduced 'Belle Isis' in 1845, a 1.2 m (4 ft) high shrub. The flowers have many pale-pink petals, paler at the edges. Their scent, similar to myrrh, is fairly strong.

Roses with Striped Flowers

The first bicolour roses were recent creations, and are very fashionable today. Many growers throughout the world are carrying out research into developing new varieties. Swim & Ellis has 'Double Delight', introduced in the United States by Armstrong in 1977: this is a hybrid tea rose with a lovely scent, and creamy-white petals edged in red.

In California, Ralph Moore created roses with striped flowers, combining yellow, pink, red, or white and pink.

In France, Delbard introduced 'Pinocchio' and 'Claude Monet', which have sold widely.

'Ingrid Bergman'® rose *poulman*, Poulsen Roser Aps.

Meilland created 'Chacock' and 'Gypsie'. In 1988, Ogilvie introduced 'Festival Fanfare' to the

'Claude Monet'® roses *jacdesa* Delbard.

United States, a sport (hybrid) of the *floribunda* 'Fred Loads', a widely marketed rose. It has pink flowers with white stripes and a light scent and is perpetual flowering.

In New Zealand, McGredy produced 'Regensberg', 'Buffalo Bill' and 'Young Mistress', these frothy and compact *floribundas*, 60 cm (2 ft) high, have double pale-pink flowers with crimson tints, and shades of white at the base of the petals. Good continuous flowering, pleasantly scented.

Centre: Garden of Anne-Marie Grivaz, Lardy.

Below: Mary-Fairchild Mac Monnies, *Roses and Lilies*. Musée des Beaux-Arts, Rouen.

Below right: Climbing rose 'New Dawn' and *Campanula latifolia*, Wisley.

Simplicity is the Best Guarantee of Good Taste

An exemplary way to apply the rules of simplicity would be to combine an old-fashioned rose bush, climbing up a stone wall, with stinking hellebores (*Helleborus foetidus*). Rose bushes with yellow flowers only look good in front of a screen of greenery, particularly if it is blueish

Garden Roses

A single rose bush can become the focal point of a garden, depending on what species is used, its shape and flowering time. Grouped in clumps, they can fill up a space. Climbers can cover, decorate and conceal unattractive areas... Rose bushes can also be thought of as a self-contained element in a garden's layout.

plants with bright-red, orangey-red or deep-red flowers or foliage: salvias (*Salvia elegans*); cannas (*Canna indica*); red-flowering lobelias; fuchsias (*Fuchsia magellanica*); rose bushes (*Rosa moyesii* and 'Frensham'); red dahlias; 'Black Knight' buddleia; red-flowering laurels; red geraniums; the purple foliage of the 'Purpurea' cordyline;

green, like some conifers. Place them next to santolinas and certain almond-green grasses, or the bright-green or striated foliage of cordylines.

Going for Red

Do not forget to mix red rose bushes with other

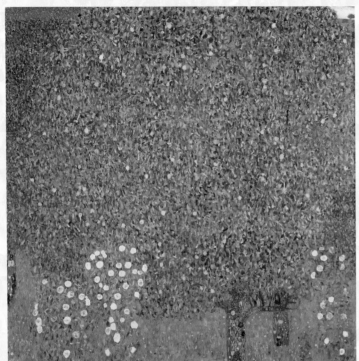

Gustav Klimt,
*Rose Bushes
beneath Trees*.
Musée d'Orsay,
Paris.

• Plant and leave a blue-flowering clematis to climb into a climbing rose with pink flowers, and plant lavender beneath it. You will love the divine scents that this combination will release. Lavender likes dry

Solray,
La Roseraie,
15 February 1904.
Coll. Arch. Dép. 94.

red peonies; small maples with red and bronze foliage ... not to mention statues, basins, terracotta pots and grey stone urns to complete the scene.

A Great Classic in Blue
• Combine pink roses in a clump with delphiniums and larkspur in shades of blue.
• You can mix all perennial roses with blue flowers. Set them against shades of green, especially those with evergreen foliage (box, ivy, yew, conifers and certain grasses, etc.).

Clematis and *Rosa banksiae lutea*.

ground and is not fond of water; so it will not impede the rose bush, which is always thirsty in summer.

• Combine *Ceanothus impressus* with bush roses or climbers with pink flowers; it is simple to do and they grow well.

Going for White

• Beneath a fragrant white-flowering climbing rose, plant white irises,

white lilies, white dahlias and anthemis.

• Behind low-growing roses you can plant a syringa with double white flowers, a Mexican orange tree with

Rosa banksiae lutea
on a balustrade.

Below:
Artist unknown, engraving with roses. Coll. Arch. Dép. 94.

Opposite:
'Fée des Neiges' rose, *Choysia, Delphinium, Veronica*. Private garden in Belgium.

white flowers (these bloom three times a year), an osmanthus (that will flower before the roses) or a lavatera with pink-white flowers.

• Place a climbing rose together with a 'Blanc de Coubert' clematis.

Growing Roses in Pots

Many rose bushes that are fragile, or sensitive to severe cold, can be grown in pots. You can also take them indoors to protect them in the winter.

Ground-cover roses look very attractive in basins. Choose perpetual-flowering creeping or pliable species for your terrace and plant them in May; they will flower throughout the summer. The rose bush should be planted alone in a pot, and mixed with other plants in a basin.

Roses in pots do not like drying out and may lose their buds, so they should be watered carefully.

Water the soil directly and, from time to time, add a little liquid fertiliser to the water. During the flowering period, roses need little feeding; stop adding fertiliser at the end of summer.

• Plant a ground-cover rose bush to decorate a stone wall, and above it place a white-flowering wistaria.

A Feast of the Senses

For a really sensual display, plant *Achemilla mollis* beneath *Rosa rugosa*, and rose bushes with floral and fruity, spicy and musky scents. To add a note of orange, how about planting some rhubarb or winter cherries?

Choosing Your Roses

There are so many varieties of roses, it can be very difficult to choose the right one to plant in a garden, on a terrace or in a pot on the balcony of an apartment. Learn how to choose between vigorous climbers, standard roses, country roses, bush roses with dense foliage, small roses to plant in a pot or as ground cover.

Detail from a drawing by Paul Berton showing a young married couple. Coll. Arch. Dép. 94.

Rich Adornments for Hedges and Fences

Here is a selection of the best roses to make a fragrant hedge, decorate a fence or the side of a wall, and make lovely bouquets with hybrids of *Rosa wichuraiana* and *Rosa multiflora*.

• 'American Pillar': *R. setigera*; a very hardy rose; only flowers once, in summer. Single crimson-pink flowers.

• 'Albertine': *R. wichuraiana* × 'Mrs A.R. Waddell'; vigorous climbing rose, flowers well, not perpetual. Salmon to coppery-pink flowers; rich, penetrating scent.

• 'May Queen': *R. wichuraiana* × 'Champion of the World'; climbs on sheds; fragrant.

Rosa wichuraiana 'Synstylse' (1981).

• 'Albéric Barbier': *R. wichuraiana* × 'Shirley Hibbard'; climber with ivory-white flowers and pale-ochre heart; strong scent.

• 'Auguste Gervais': *R. wichuraiana* × 'Le Progrès'; climber with pinkish-white flowers; heady scent.

A Matter of Height: Weeping Standard Roses

Weeping rose bushes are obtained by grafting a creeping rose onto a standard rose, often supported by a metal stake with a parasol cover. There are several heights for this kind of rose bush:

Miniature: 50 cm (1.5 ft); suitable for small terraces and balconies.
Half-standard: 75 cm (2.5 ft); suitable for clumps and corners of small gardens.
Standard: 1.2 to 1.5 m (4 to 5 ft); the best height for showing off weeping roses.

• 'Bleu Magenta': multiflora; unknown origin.
climber with delicate, delightful crimson flowers with golden stamens; fragrant.

Elegant and Sumptuous Standard Roses

The Bagatelle rose garden, associated with the Jules Gravereaux rose garden at L'Haÿ-les-Roses, has beautiful stands of standard roses, aligned to create magnificent border effects, exhibited in a clump or grown in rows of pots.
• 'Paul Noël': hybrid of *R. wichuraiana*; magnificent weeping standard rose with salmon-pink flowers tending towards fuchsia-red as they fade, little scent.
• 'Rosary', 'Roserie': climbing hybrid of *R. multiflora*; best seen at L'Haÿ-les-Roses.
• 'Red Cascade': climbing rose with small bright-red, profuse flowers.

Dashing Climbers

Marvellous and enchanting rose bushes that shoot up façades, cover dead trees, decorate arches and run along skilfully placed trellises...
• 'Bobbie James': hybrid of *R. multiflora*: very vigorous climber with bright sturdy foliage, covered with large clusters of single, white, bowl-shaped and very fragrant flowers. Ideal for covering old trees.
• 'Alchemist': modern climbing hybrid, medium height; double fawn-yellow flowers with orangey shades; strong scent. Not perpetual.
• 'Mermaid': *R. bracteata* × tea rose; vigorous climber with fragrant single yellow flowers, magnificent intense-green foliage, almost perpetual.

Weeping standard rose 'Excelsa', Bagatelle.

'Mermaid' rose.

• 'American Pillar': hybrid of *R. wichuraiana*; up to 6 m (20 ft) high; elongated glossy leaves, crimson-pink flowers with white buds. Like the white eglantine. Not perpetual.

Bushes Where Birds Love to Perch

Nightingales, tits, blackbirds and chaffinches fight over the protective, fragrant shelter of rose bushes in gardens and vines where these vigorous bushes flower, some of them spiny, others with very soft foliage ... not forgetting the great country rose bushes and the ground-cover plants, which are happy to scale the roof of a shed.

• 'Yvonne Rabier': hybrid of *polyantha* with shiny leaves.

• 'Blanc Double de Coubert': very perpetual hybrid of *R. rugosa*; figured foliage and lovely pure-white, bowl shaped flowers.

• 'Le Vésuve', 'Lemesle': very spiny China rose.

• 'Prosperity': musky hybrid with tall curving stems.

• 'Dentelle de Malines': modern shrub; flowers once.

• 'Swany': large country rose bush with small white flowers, slightly fragrant.

Border of Delbard roses.

• 'Fiona': ground-covering rose bush with large fragrant crimson-red flowers.

• 'Tumbling Waters': small bush up to 60 to 80 cm (2 to 2.5 ft); low growing,

'Lavender Dream'® *interlav* Delbard.

dense and sturdy; small double white flowers in clusters, strongly scented.

Reviving the Art of Planting in Clumps

Great efforts and imaginative feats have been made by towns and villages in recent years to plant in clumps, leading to simple displays and smart colours. These new roses have proved themselves in municipal and private displays. They are usually hardy; when planted close together in numbers, they create an interesting effect of mass in the landscape. Small bushes and, more recently, miniature roses are more and more sought after for gardens.

• 'Pompom de Paris': China rose 60 cm (2 ft) high; available as a climber, light scent.

• 'The Fairy': *polyantha* ground-cover rose with pink flowers, 60 cm (2 ft) high and 1.2 m (4 ft) wide. Continuous flowering.

'Bordur Vive'® *delboviv* Delbard.

• 'Pink Bells': rose bush 60 cm (2 ft) high and 1.2 m (4 ft) wide, produced by Poulsen. Delicate pink colour.

The 'Coeur Farouche' rose bush, a favourite in gardens.

• 'Bonica': very profuse rose 1 m (3 ft) high × 1.5 m (5 ft) wide, produced by Meilland. Pink flowers, slight scent; resistant to diseases.

• 'Lavender Dream': pretty, small modern shrub 60 cm (2 ft) high with mauve flowers, produced by Interplant-Delbard (France).

Perpetual; very profuse but slight scent.

• 'Tango': rose bush 60 cm (2 ft) high. Light-red flowers with yellow heart, fragrant.

• 'Palace': collection created by Poulsen (Denmark), bringing together 14 superb small rose bushes for clumps, basins and window boxes.

• 'Droming Margrethe Palace': small bush 40 to 60 cm (1.5 to 2 ft) high. Many double pompom flowers; fresh scent, dark shiny foliage.

A Rose by Any Other Name

Rose, Rosa, Rosalie, Rosalind, Rosalinde, Rosamund, Rose-Marie, Rosemary, Rosette, Rosie, Rosine, Rosita, Roxana, Marie-Rose

Exquisite Miniatures

Roses growing less than 60 cm (2 ft) high are called 'miniature roses'. Ralph Moore, in particular, has produced marvellous miniatures in California. The very famous Poulsen nursery introduced a very diverse group of ground-cover roses, including the well-known 'Kent'. However, it should not be thought that miniature roses are a recent creation: they have been around for a long time.

'Pompom de Bougogne' is a *centifolia* known in France since 1664 and grown in pots. The descendants of a China rose called 'Roulettii' showed

Terrasse de l'Amour at the L'Haÿ-les-Roses rose garden.

Detail from a poster by the Horticultural and Viticultural Society of Epernay, created for the inauguration of its garden, 4 September 1910. Coll. Arch. Dép. 94.

the way for new bushes of this type, with almost perfectly formed flowers, and bright and original colours, which can be mixed together. In 1985, Tom Carruth created the miniature 'Heart Breaker' with creamy flowers edged in pink.

'Iceberg' rose.

Varieties for Carpets of Colour

• 'Cherry Magic': miniature rose 60 cm (2 ft) high. Soft red flowers.
• 'Scarlet Moss': miniature moss rose 50 cm (1.5 ft) high with intense-red flowers.
• 'Mandarin': tiny bush (30 cm/1 ft high), very profuse with large pink flowers and a golden heart.
• 'Minijet': delicate miniature rose with pale-pink flowers, created by Meilland in France in 1977.
• 'Charming Palace': a recent Poulsen creation; miniature rose for growing in pots, with semi-double, pure-red flowers and glossy, dark foliage; light scent.

Song for a Rose

Quite simply
like a rose
That one picks one day
for no reason
You have taken my troubled heart
Just going past
my house

It's Raining Roses

Cascades and constellations
of roses on walls, bowers and
arches, in hanging baskets;
the opulence of weeping
standard roses...
• 'Auguste Gervais':
R. wichuraiana × 'Le Progrès';
climber with large pink-white
flowers; pleasant scent.
• 'Nozomie': superb weeping
standard rose with miniature
flowers, produced by
Onodera in Japan (1968).
If trained, it can climb.
• 'Sweet Chariot': perpetual
miniature rose with clusters
of red flowers, produced
by Moore in the United
States in 1984. Ideal in
a hanging basket.

Stellenberg Manor, South Africa.

Unusual Roses

A rose can be unusual in terms of its shape, the colour of its petals, its scent, the colour of the wood, the presence of many large spines (or their absence), the bush's silhouette, the colour of the hips, its evergreen foliage, its coarse leaves...

Rosa moyesii geranium.

From the Simplest Shapes to the Weirdest

Large spread-out or curving bowls, flowers closed in on themselves, strange petals...
• *Rosa moyesii*: a rose with bright-red flowers and numerous rounded leaflets.
• 'Reine Victoria': a Bourbon rose with curving flowers.

Clashing Colours

Strong colours impose themselves, making us forget the more delicately coloured roses. Whether we like them or not, we cannot remain indifferent to them.
• 'The Pilgrim': English rose with flowers in a soft shade of yellow turning to white at the edges.
• 'Viridiflora': *R. chinensis* var. *viridiflora*; green roses! They are a mutation of *R. chinensis* 'Old Blush' whose petals, stamens and pistils have become transformed with greenish strips.

Many-coloured Roses, a Rainbow Parade

Old-fashioned roses with splashes of pink came before the modern so-called 'striped' roses.
• *Rosa gallica* 'Versicolor': a sport of the Provins rose. A many-coloured rose called 'Rosa Mundi' after the name of Henry II of England's favourite, Rosamund, who died in 1176.

Bourbon rose 'Reine Victoria', created by Schwartz in 1872.

Rosa viridiflora.

- 'Tricolore de Flandre':
a rose created in Belgium by
Van Houtte in 1846. Beautiful
white roses streaked with
pink.
- 'Honorine de Brabant':
a large Bourbon rose.

'L'Africaine'
rose.

The Black Rose
There is, almost, a black rose.
Meilland created one, 'Fuego
Negro', with petals of such a
dark crimson that they seem
black; the black actually
came from an accumulation
of crimson pigments
(cynadiol). This rose is also
remarkable for its velvety
petals. The richness of its
texture is set off by deep

glints. When it fades, bronze
highlights appear on the
corolla, around the petals.

Nasty Scents
Our main notion of the
scent of roses is a pleasant
one, and this prevents us
from imagining that there
may be roses with an
unpleasant scent. The idea
is so upsetting that we do
not want to think about it.
A rose smelling like a bug?
Yes, indeed. Try the
Capuchin roses 'Persian
Yellow' and *Rosa banksiae*

'Honorine de Brabant' rose.

lutea. A tarragon smell?
Try the 'Eugénie Lamesch' ...
a rose for the kitchen. A smell
of leather? There are three:
'Clément Nabonnand', 'Mme
Ch. Genoud' and 'Souvenir
d'Espagne'.

Moonstone Roses
The so-called blue roses
have a number of colours
which vary with the available
light: lilac, blueish-white,
metallic white, violet,
blue shading to violet,
mother-of-pearl white,
and pure white with pinkish
and blueish glints. There
are roses with mother-of-
pearl-blue petals like
certain sky colours.
Others reduce us to silence
by the weight of their scent.
They hint of the magic of
moonstones in the depths
of the earth.
- 'Blue Girl': climbing hybrid
tea rose, introduced in 1974.
Gently fragrant.
- 'Shocking Blue': *floribunda*
(seedling × 'Silver Star'), a
bush up to 80 cm (2.5 ft)

Nature as Artist or Nature as Sorceress

A rose that grows in a rose! This curious phenomenon is thought to be caused by a deficiency of trace elements, occuring in the *centifolia* species in the rose garden at L'Haÿ-les-Roses (Val-de-Marne). We wonder if, in the long term, this could produce a genetic mutation. The gardeners at the rose garden, who have observed this phenomenon regularly, may be able to give us an answer.

high. Lovely flowers with a tinge of violet. Flowers all summer; pleasant scent.
• 'Charles de Gaulle': ('Sissi' × 'Prelude') × ('Kordes Sondermeldung' × 'Caprice'); a rose with a delicate floral scent, introduced in 1974.
• 'Seven Seas': *floribunda* bush up to 80 cm (2.5 ft) high; bowl-shaped, blueish-pink flowers, pleasant scent.
• 'Blue Moon', 'Blue Monday', 'Sissi', 'Mainzer Fastnacht': hybrid teas 80 cm

(2.5 ft) high. Blue colouring. Flower all summer. Divine scent.
• 'Sterling Silver': hybrid tea 60 cm (2 ft) high, introduced in 1957. Silvery-lilac flowers, gentle scent. Not for cold climates.
• 'Lagerfeld', 'Starlight': hybrid tea 80 cm (2.5 ft) high. Violet-grey flowers and light scent.
• 'Mamy Blue Del Blue' (Delbard): bush rose 80 cm to 1 m (2.5 ft to 3 ft) high, good spread, profuse and disease resistant. Large double flowers in mauve with blueish glints. Strong scent.
• 'L'Evêque' (syn. 'The Bishop'): upright *R. gallica* 90 cm to 1.3 m (3 ft to 4 ft) high, remarkable for its vigorous dark-green foliage. Lovely rosette-type double flowers in magenta-red shading to

Rosa 'Blue Moon' (hybrid tea rose).

violet-grey with blueish tones at the end of the season. Flowers once in June.

The Mystery of Blue Roses
In the 12th century, the botanist Ibn el-Awam described in his now-rare work *Kitab al felebah* the artificial process for obtaining blue roses: 'These roses were obtained by using indigo. The bark was removed from the

'Christian Lacroix' rose, designed by Christian Lacroix and created by Truffaut in 1999.

roots and stems of the rose plant [a double white rose, probably *Rosa moschata* var. double] and the powder, ground up in a mortar, was inserted between the sapwood and the bark. It was tied up, replanted in the ground and watered.' Later they inserted 'strong blue B' or 'acid violet 10 B' into the same

'Christian Lacroix' roses, created by Truffaut.

white-flowering plant; and it absorbed these chemical salts. Today, genetic engineers have still not managed to make genetic modifications.

Surprising Foliage

• *Rosa willmottiae*: China rose introduced in 1904. It has long flexible stems more than 2 m (6 ft) high, but its foliage consists of tiny feather-light leaves.
• 'Rosier à Feuilles de Laitue': the origins of this rose are unknown. It appeared around the 16th century, but was not listed until 1801 (*centifolia* syn./ 4 *Rosa* × *centifolia* 'Bullata'). Its unusual foliage is large, drooping, creased and puffy like lettuce leaves, with a hint of red when young. The flowers are pink, double, with glandulous peduncles. Not perpetual; 1.2 m (4 ft) high.
• *Rosa carolina*: superb North American shrub with large supple stems and bright foliage, magnificent in autumn with its red colours and globular hips; 1 m to 1.5 m (3 ft to 4.5 ft) high.

Aromatic Leaves

The leaves of these roses have small glands that release

The Painters' Roses

Delbard, who no doubt loves painting, created 'Henri Matisse', 'Camille Pissarro', 'Paul Cézanne' and 'Claude Monet', rose bushes with large flowers or clusters of flowers.

'Paul Cézanne'® roses, *jacdeli*, Delbard.

perfume. They are really nice. Place them near paths in the garden and rub a leaf between your fingers as you go by.
• 'Lord Penzance': medium climbing eglantine, with delicate scented foliage of green apple. Single yellow flowers, pinkish at the edges, followed by red hips. Not perpetual.
• 'Rosa Primula': rose from China and Central Asia also known as 'Incense Rose',

because of the scent of incense on its very fine foliage. Small pale primrose-yellow flowers. Not perpetual.

• 'Amy Robsart': hybrid of *R. rubiginosa* (scented eglantine) with graceful, pink flowers. The foliage has an exquisite scent of apple.

The Smallest Rose

Rosa yakushimanense, from the name Yaku-shima, the small island in the extreme south of Japan which it comes from, bears tiny white flowers with yellow stamens; it has very vigorous branches, protected by numerous fine spines. A rapid grower.

Rosa primula, Chelsea Physic Garden.

Decorative and Tasty Rose Hips

They are lovely to look at in autumn and in a winter frost, and are

Rosa 'Bullata'.

good to eat as a kind of jam or condiment, with their fruity, peppery, musky flavours.

• *Rosa roxburghii* *Rosa roxburghii* f. *normalis* (known as the chestnut rose): a strange rose with hips covered in spines like the fruits of the chestnut.

• *Roa moyesii*: rose with very spectacular red, elongated, bottle-shaped hips.

A Treat to Eat!

You must know the rosehips of the eglantines, full of vitamin C and used to make fresh jams, but there are some other rosehips that are well worth trying. Gently remove the hips, then cook them like condiments or fruits. Dry the driest ones or grind them to a powder, and make jam with the sweetest ones.

• *Rosa corymbefera gallica*: round, full-bodied, bright-red hips with a soft pulp. Flavours of apricot and honey.

Rosa rugosa follis.

• *Rosa carolina glandulosa*: small, long, elegant, orangey-red fruits with a thin, fairly dry pulp. Spicy flavours of incense and myrtle.

• *Rosa pimpinellifolia* 'William II' (*R. sulphurea*): the fruits are like plump black-violet blackcurrants, the flesh soft. Flavour of blackcurrant.

• *Rosa alba*: plump, pulpy, full-bodied fruits, elongated in shape with soft flesh. Spicy flavour like the flesh of cooked tomato.

• *Rosa setipoda cinnamomeae*: bright-red fruits, elongated in shape, little flesh. Flavour of exotic fruit (persimmon).

Weapons or Attractions?
Saint-Exupéry's Little Prince would have been very happy to have had a rose without thorns, but the one he was looking after certainly did not have spines like these...

Rosa omeinsis.

Rosa sericea f. *pteracantha* is a rose grown as a curiosity for its enormous wing-like spines, which in spring are joined by tiny fragile white flowers. The spines are quite arresting when looked at against the light.

White Roses to Wave in the Wind
There are fields of white roses which wave in the summer wind. Dense bushes covered with clusters of pure white, which conceal black beetles.

• 'Mousseline', 'Alfred de Dalmas': perpetual damask moss rose with

Rosa myriacantha. The rose with a thousand spines. Coll. Arch. Dép. 94.

a pleasant scent, 1.2 m (4 ft) high.

• 'Iceberg (Climbing)': a climbing rose ('Robin Hood × 'Virgo') with a profusion of almost double, pure-white flowers in

'Summer Snow Climbing', a *polyantha* hybrid.

large clusters, 5 m (16 ft) high.

• 'White Dawn': a climbing rose ('New Dawn' × 'Lily Pons') with a sophisticated scent, 4 m (13 ft) high.

• 'Summer Snow Climbing': *floribunda* grown by Cocteau in 1936; 2 m (6 ft) high.

• 'Crystalline': hybrid tea rose with pure-white flowers.

Great Rose Gardens

The great rose lovers have created Gardens of Eden by growing and displaying roses in a splendid number of varieties alongside sculptures, fountains and pools, and the birds that live there, lovely trellises and green hedges, music, and so on. These great gardens can be found in abbeys, châteaux and city parks. Some are formal rose garens, real natural conservatories, lovingly protected. These gardens of paradise can be visited in the summer months.

Rose Gardens in France

Roses have been grown in France since Charlemagne. In the Middle Ages, roses were a favourite flower for walled gardens. At Malmaison, Joséphine de Beauharnais brought together all the roses known at that time. Roses were even produced in abbeys.

Ancient spectacle put on in Jules Gravereaux's lifetime at the rose garden of L'Haÿ-les-Roses. Coll. Arch. Dép. 94.

The Rose Garden at L'Haÿ-les-Roses in the Val-du-Marne

It was created in 1899 by Jules Gravereaux on 15,000 square metres (18,000 square yards) of land. The Département de la Seine opened the rose garden, after it had been restored, in 1939. Today it is managed by the Département du Val-de-Marne. This huge conservatory with its massive greenhouses is unquestionably the most important rose garden in Europe, and perhaps in the world, by virtue of its ancient collections. In 1910, the collection had up to 8,000 rose bushes and trees, and today has 3,300 cultivars (including 182 botanical species) and other varieties, with 85% of the roses created before 1950. There are more than 16,000 plants. The rose garden also has many species collected by Jules Gravereaux.

The Rose Garden in the Botanical Gardens at Nancy

This rose garden was built in 1997 with the help of André Eve, and tells the fabulous history of roses. It has 1,400 rose bushes, planted in chronological order according to when they were discovered or created, amounting to 270 species and horticultural varieties.

The Rose Garden in the Jardin des Plantes at Clermont-Ferrand

Created in 1925, this rose garden has period pergolas weighed down with roses. There is also a botanical garden, an open-air theatre, sculptures and landscaped areas.

The Rose Gardens in the Parc de la Tête-d'Or, in Lyon

On the initiative of the City of Lyon, four rose gardens were created in the Parc de la Tête-d'Or, making it the city of 100,000 roses. The botanical garden has an area of 1,600 square metres (1,900 square yards) and tells the history of roses with 570 varieties in chronological order.

Opposite top: Poster for a horticultural exhibition of 1910. 'Bagatelle roses at home for almost nothing – Bagatelle and its gardens' (detail). Coll. Arch. Dép. 94.

Great Rose Gardens • 69

Above: Rose garden in the Parc de la Tête-d'Or, Lyon.

The International Rose Garden, created in 1961 and opened in 1964, covers 50 hectares (120 acres) and shows 60,000 rose bushes from 320 old-fashioned and modern varieties. It is laid out in a green bower beside the lake.

Previous pages: Private rose garden of André Eve, Pithiviers.

Left and right: Water garden and flower garden at Claude Monet's house at Giverny. Fondation Claude-Monet, Giverny.

Remarkable Roses at L'Haÿ-les-Roses

• The white York rose: known since Antiquity; grows wild in Kurdistan.
• The Provins rose, Apothecary's rose, and the red rose of Lancaster: ancestors of cultivated roses.
• The musk rose: not found in nature, comes from the Near East.
• Capuchin rose: originally from Asia Minor, unusual colour.
• Scented eglantines, rust-coloured roses: vigorous wild roses, flowers with a scent of Cox or Reinette apples.
• Moss rose: mutation of *R. centifolia*, appeared at Carcassonne in 1696.
• China rose with green flowers: strange example of natural mutation.
• 'Madame Caroline Testout': named after a famous Paris milliner; lovely pointed buds.
• 'Soleil d'Or': first hybrid of the yellow tea rose.
• Ramanas rose: hardy rose; magnificent shrub with crimson-pink flowers and large red hips.
• Banksian rose with yellow flowers.

Chivalry and Roses at Bagatelle

Bagatelle is a historic wooden house in the Bois de Boulogne, Paris. Originally, it was an 18th-century folly created in 1777 by the Comte d'Artois (who became Charles X). The delightful Madame d'Estrées organised amorous and licentious events in the elegant house, where eminent courtiers gathered. Bagatelle was spared by the Revolution and later became the hunting lodge of Napoleon I, then of the Duc de Berry. Bagatelle went through an English phase, when its park was redesigned by the landscape designer Varé. Bagatelle has been owned by the City of Paris since 1905, It was then given a rose garden on the initiative of J.C.N. Forestier. Several hundred species of roses were supplied by Jules Gravereaux from the rose garden at L'Haÿ.

RÉPUBLIQUE FRANÇAISE
VILLE DE PARIS

CONCOURS INTERNATIONAL
DE
ROSES NOUVELLES
DE BAGATELLE
1907-1932

Rose Garden of the Abbey of Fontfroide

This Cistercian abbey nestles in the hills of

Corbières, and looks most impressive and serene. Around the church's cloister and the many buildings, there are thousands of roses: 2,300 plants, giving 11 intense and brilliant colour variations, arranged in blocks running from red to white via apricot. Borders of box and santolinas with blueish foliage bring out these colours, which are set off against a background of hills and scrubland.

Opposite background:
Spectacle put on in Jules Gravereaux's lifetime at the rose garden of L'Haÿ-les-Roses. Coll. Arch. Dép. 94.

Opposite bottom:
Artist unknown, *Rose trellis*. Coll. Arch. Dép. 94.

Right:
Kiosk of the Empress, Bagatelle rose garden. The Bagatelle rose garden is in a pure French style with sober lines, and displays a magnificent collection of roses, presenting a wonderful variety of ancient and modern species: 1,000 varieties and 9,500 roses grown from *polyanthas*, *floribundas*, hybrid tea roses, climbers, standard roses and weeping roses.

English Rose Gardens

The natural English style, with its park sloping gently down to a lake, its old house or church glimpsed between clumps of trees, the whole surrounded by neighbouring hills, has made its mark on the art of gardens and our imagination.

Close-up of clumps of 'Celsiana' roses in summer. Garden of Mottisfont Abbey, Hampshire.

'Warwick Castle'

This flower is one of the most representative English roses, with its geometric corolla and many petals, and its transparent intense pink colour lit by a touch of flame. It is richly scented, with gently arching branches and grows to 80 cm (2.5 ft) high.

Ancient and Modern

Rose gardens were laid out in sheltered corners, between clumps of shrubs, and planted with a variety of rose bushes separated by small wire arches. Roses from China were imported around 1790. The hybrids were planted in among the oldest bushes of damask, York and Lancaster roses.

The Gardens of the Rose, the Royal National Rose Society

This is an impressive collection of 30,000 roses grown in a magnificent setting. These classified and listed roses cover every period since the 15th century. There are also some of the oldest wild roses, and delicate miniature roses. Part of the garden is set aside for researchers and botanists planting new creations which have not yet been marketed.

Royal Presidents

The first great national rose exhibition took place at St James's Hall, Piccadilly in London. The gardens were presided over by Her Majesty Queen Alexandra from 1885 to 1925, then by Her Majesty Queen Mary, and from 1955 until her death in 2002, by Elizabeth the Queen Mother.

Left:
Rose garden at Sissinghurst Castle, Kent.

Background:
View of the tower of Sissinghurst Castle above clumps of roses.

Below:
Captivating summer scene of pink rose bushes, and pergolas covered in climbing roses with pink and red flowers. Mottisfont Abbey, Hampshire.

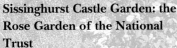

Sissinghurst Castle Garden: the Rose Garden of the National Trust

The land was originally occupied by a medieval manor house. In 1930, the novelist and poet Vita Sackville-West bought the property, restored the surviving buildings and created one of the most beautiful gardens in England. The Rose Garden has such a variety of sweet-scented and remarkably beautiful flowers, it attracts crowds of visitors every year.

Right:
Charles-Paul Renouard, *Portrait of Jules Gravereaux in the Rose Garden at L'Haÿ-les-Roses*. Coll. Arch. Dép. 94.

Opposite:
Antoine Meilland.

Rose Lovers

*R*ose lovers make up a vast worldwide family consisting of growers, enlightened amateurs, gardeners and perfumers. They meet up at conferences and all kinds of events: rose festivals, awards and prize-giving ceremonies for growers, the launch of new roses, and so on. The most passionate specialists have left their mark on the history of roses.

Jules Gravereaux

Jules Gravereaux formerly worked for the Bon Marché stores in Paris, then from 1892 this committed rose enthusiast devoted his life to forming a collection of roses, which he planted at his property in L'Haÿ, near Paris. He collected roses from all round the world, and in five years brought together more than 1,600 cultivars, and wild and ancient roses. In 1899, Edouard André, his nurseryman, laid out the first rose garden in France.

Antoine Meilland

As a child, Antoine Meilland was struck by the roses of his neighbour, Mme Rivière. She told him the story of Redouté

and gave him a budding knife. He decided to become a rose grower and worked for the horticulturist Dubreuil, marrying his daughter, Claudia. He then worked furiously to build a real collection, beginning with 'Gloire de Dijon'. Despite encountering difficulties, he managed to gather more than 20,000 rose bushes grafted onto wild plants found in the forest. On a visit to the engineer Mallerin, accompanied by his son Francis, he discovered a golden-yellow rose with glossy green foliage, and this determined his young son's vocation. Francis's first hybrid was made from 'Sunstar' (a semi-double scented red rose) and 'Sir David Davis' (a deep-crimson double rose). Thus the legend of the Meillands began. Some of their roses are still famous: 'Happiness' (1949) and Baccara' (1955).

Baccara var. meger rose.

Francis Meilland fought to obtain exclusive patents on the new cultivars then being recognised in Europe.

Nanda d'Ursel

Around 1950, Countess Nanda d'Ursel took over the running of the gardens of the Château de Hex, near Liège in Belgium. The discovery of old-fashioned roses at the far end of the property gave her a great passion for roses. Today, the arbours of the rose garden contain a balanced selection of many

old-fashioned species, some of them difficult to obtain: *Rosa moschata*; *Rosa primula*, whose small flowers have a scent of incense; *Rosa gallica versicolor*; 'Paul's Himalayan Musk'; 'Alain Blanchard'; and 'Weichenblau', with its violet flowers.

David Austin

In England, at the beginning of the 1960s, David Austin stunned the gardening world by creating a new family of scented roses which he called 'English roses'. These were the result of crossing perpetual, hardy roses and old-fashioned roses, chosen for their more graceful bearing, the refined beauty of their shapes, their delicate colours and incomparable perfumes. The English roses delighted all those nostalgic for perfumed roses at a time when many roses were being marketed which were certainly magnificent but had no scent.

Rose Gardens in Northern Europe

The countryside going north from the Ardennes plateau offers a series of age-old forests and deep valleys. Peat marshes and luxuriant meadows full of meditating cows give way to plains swept by wind, rain and snow.

Some of Poulsen's Prize-winning Roses

'Bournonville', 'Princess Alexandra', 'Clair Renaissance', 'Easy Cover', 'Schackenborg', 'White Cover', 'Ragtime', 'Ingrid Bergman', 'Queen Margethe Palace', 'Karen Blixen', 'Courage', 'Tivoli 150', 'Flora Danica', 'Kalmar', 'Renaissance Rose'.

The Château de Hex, in Belgium

In the 18th century, Charles François de Velbruck, bishop prince of Liège, chose the undulating countryside of La Hesbaye, in Limburg, to realise an 'Arcadian dream'. He built the Château de Hex, with its English-style park and many gardens: the rose garden, the Pas-de-l'Ane meadow, the Chinese garden, the Prince's garden, the Vegetable garden and the Bee garden. This paradise on earth became his summer residence.

Handel Werbung, advertising poster for Liebig, 1895.

The Poulsen Rose Garden in Denmark

In the land of Nils and the wild geese, acres of fields are planted with small rose bushes in lively bright colours. They stretch as far as the eye can see beneath lavender-blue skies. Thousands of miniature roses in pots, each with its label, thrive in the warmth of immense greenhouses, waiting to be sent all over the world. For the last 120 years, 330 new varieties of rose plants have been created, 17 of which have won prizes. These modern roses have carried off more than 15 awards and gold medals.

Thierry Bosquet, *Château de Hex, Former Summer Residence of the Bishop Prince of Liège*, 1985. Private Collection, Belgium. Every year, in June, during the Rose Festival, European rosarians present their latest plants in the courtyard of the château. To add to its attraction, the event is backed up by a prizegiving, exhibitions and a garden party.

Below:
'Reine Margrethe' rose from the Poulsen company's gardens at Fredensborg, Denmark.

In the Land of the Valkyries

• **Palmengarten Rosen** (the palm garden) at Frankfurt-am-Main is a magnificent winter garden, created in 1846 by Adolf von Nassau. He collected more than 1,000 species of plants. The rose garden began in 1869 and was extended until 1886. More recently, under the leadership of Max Brome, the park was embellished with illuminations, competitions and concerts. Today it has a remarkable collection of old-fashioned roses and countless hybrids.

• **Planten un Blomen**, the rose garden at Hamburg. Around the lovely Apothecary's garden are wonderful fountains and romantic cascades. Strolling beside the magnificent displays of flowers, renewed every season, you will find a pretty rose garden, enhanced by its kiosk and arches.

The Marvellous Skies of Spain and Italy

Roses praised by Homer, impassioned poems which profoundly influenced our culture. There is scarcely a garden without its rose collection, from the gardens of Pliny the Younger to the Villa Hadriana at Tibur, now Tivoli, and the Marius Lucretius house at Pompeii. Roses at the Alhambra thrive beside pools... The gardens of Spain and Italy awaken our desire for paradise.

The Villa Capponi.

Wild and Passionate Spain

This sunny land seems enveloped by the heavy, sensual scent of jasmine, myrtle, orange blossom and roses. Like those other exotic shrubs, roses also came from the Near East. They were cultivated and cared for by emirs and praised by the troubadours who lived there and dreamed of love and paradise.

The Gardens of the Alhambra (Spain)

Close to the bustling city of Grenada, the murmuring waters of fountains blend with birdsong and reveal the silence of the roses. Around the box hedges, near the pools, rose bushes add their perfection to this enchanting place, once home of the Moorish kings in the 14th and 15th centuries. Charles V

increased the magnificence of the buildings with his Italian-style palace. The gardens, facing the snowy peaks of the Sierra Nevada, are magnificent.

La Ninfa (Italy)

The garden of Professor Fineschi is located north of Rome, at the foot of the Apennines. It is a marvellous romantic garden, with a collection of old-fashioned roses. The park was originally laid out by an English landscape designer. Today the garden is run by a private foundation, and every year opens its gates to the public.

Villa Capponi (Italy)

Its architecture has remained intact since the 15th century. Three secret gardens, on the Florentine hills, make up this floral paradise surrounded by high crenellated walls. Visits are by appointment.

Jardin Collavini (Italy)

This garden is in the Friule region. It has a collection of old-fashioned roses, violets and begonias, and a very beautiful 17th-century orangery. Visits are by appointment.

Palazzo Patrizi – Castel Giuliano (Italy)

This marvellous setting, some 40 kilometres (25 miles) from Rome, is rich in wild flora and fauna. The rose garden, laid out by the Marqueza Umberta, is one of the finest private rose gardens in Italy.

Serenade

In the peace
of the black alley,
beneath a silver-blue sky,
The serenade has faded,
In the depths of night,
a bitter perfume.
In the silence is a slight
Lyrical fall of leaves, echoing
Couplets cast off
in the wind
Like frail roses shedding petals...
The flowering jasmine at her
window
Trembled at the grille
Hearing a tearful song
in the alley;
The old song of a gravedigger
Who, faced with
a dead woman,
Throws down his hoe,
and begins to weep.

Francisco Villaespa
(1877–1936)

Above:
The Villa Capponi.

Left:
Emile Auguste Carolus-Duran, *Rose Seller*. Coll. Arch. Dép. 94.

The Queen of Perfumes

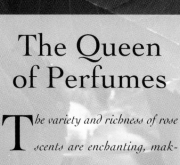

The variety and richness of rose scents are enchanting, making us forget how much these scents have been debased by industrial uses. When you add the beauty of a rose's shape and colour to its scent, it seems like a natural miracle. The rose is the queen of perfumes – a result of the many chemical compounds that are blended together, along with the composition of the soil in which roses grow and their surrounding environment.

Stunning Perfumes

The scents of roses act on our senses, our attitudes and thoughts. There is gaiety in the air, tender feelings, fresh groves, the rustling of silk taffetas and satins, the fruits of paradise, capricious moods, twilights and moonlights, a distant mirage, a promise of warm nights, an amber skin...

Above:
Dispensers for rose water, Tunisia, end of 19th century. Musée International de la Parfumerie, Grasse.

Making Rose and Chypre Perfumes in Greece

According to Theophrastes, the flowers or their petals were macerated beforehand in sweet wine with various herbs or spices. The flowers were then mixed with an oily substance (Egyptian balanite oil, bitter almond oil or omphalium). This oil was exposed to fire, though not directly, in a sort of bain-marie which concentrated the liquid without altering its nature. For chypre perfume, salt was added.

The Inventors of Rose Water and Essential Oil of Roses

The Arabs made the first distillations around 980. Their great scientist Avicenna is credited with inventing the coil to chill steam from the alembic. The discovery of essential oil of roses is also attributed to him.

A Mongolian Fantasy

In 1612, according to the annals of the country, the most sumptuous marriage ever took place between the ambitious princess Nour Djihan and the emperor Djihangugr. The princess wanted to surprise and delight her future husband and had the idea of getting rose water to flow through the canals of her garden. As they sat together in a boat moving over the perfumed waters, the emperor noticed that foam was forming at the sides of the canal. In this way, quite by chance, rose oil was discovered.

Making Essential Oil of Roses

Water saturated with rose petals is distilled to give an essential oil and rose water. The first distilling is not enough to extract the essential oil. A second distillation produces

Right and opposite bottom:
Damask roses drying in the valley of Dadès, Morocco. Roses for making perfume must be picked early in the morning, before the sun warms up. In fact, the essences evaporate if exposed to heat. A good picker harvests 30 to 40 kilos (66 to 88 lb) of petals a day, which will produce 200 grams (7 oz) of essence.

The Queen of Perfumes • 83 •

'indirect essence'. All parts of the flower contain the essential oil, but the petals hold most of all. The essential oil content is highest between seven and nine o'clock in the morning, when the temperature, humidity and sunlight are most favourable.

It takes 60,000 roses to make 30 grams (1 oz) of essential rose oil, which explains its very high price.

The Constituents of Essential Rose Oil

According to the results of the latest scientific research, the essential oil of the Bulgarian rose contains 275 elements. Among the constituents of essential rose oil having a scent of roses are citronellal, geraniol, nerol, phenylethyl alcohol and farnesol. Other constituents, in the form of trace elements, enable the olfactory miracle of rose perfume to be realised. Most of all, however, we should not forget the importance of the sun, the time of day, and the trees and shrubs growing nearby in determining the characteristics of the perfume.

Above:
Rose petal distillery. Coll. Parfumerie Fragonard, Grasse.

Right and opposite above:
Roses for perfume being treated in the valley of Dadès, Morocco.

Background:
Cover of *Treatise on Scents* by the distiller M. Déjean, 1777. Coll. Arch. Dép. 94.

The 'Concrete' and 'Absolute' Rose Essence

Extraction using an organic solvent from petroleum derivatives yields a solid substance known as a concrete, which will produce 50 to 60% of the absolute essence, the concentrated flower oil. This is used in perfumes ('extracts') and toilet waters.

Rose Water

This is a by-product of the distilling process. Rose water is sensitive to microbiological modifications; it is protected with preservatives such as para-hydroxybenozoics of methyl, ethyl or isopropyl. Ibn Chadoun, the Arab historian, reported that in the 8th and 9th centuries rose water was intensively traded from Europe to the Far East. Bulgaria, which began growing roses in 1610, is today one of the main producers of rose water.

Right:
Cardboard powder box surmounted by a porcelain female bust whose dress is covered with cloth petals, c. 1925. Musée International de la Parfumerie, Grasse.

Above right:
C.S. Hugard, *Experimental Laboratory for Testing Rose Scents*, c. 1861. Coll. Arch. Dép. 94.

Some Dates in the History of Chemistry

1894: Hesse identified citronellal in essential rose oil.

1896: Hesse, Erdmann, Bertram and Gildemeister identified geraniol in essential rose oil.

1900: Roahn noticed the presence of phenylethyl alcohol in essential oil, and demonstrated the presence of linalool.

1949: Naves found eugenol and its methylic ether.

1953: Ivanov and his collaborators studied the composition of stearoptines and the waxy elements of essential rose oil. This work still continues today.

Beauty and the Promise of Roses

The rose is an accomplice of feminine beauty ... its perfumes help to perfect their seductiveness. Since the mists of time, balms, beauty creams and scented oils have helped to maintain the freshness, beauty and youthfulness of their skins.

Beauty, a Perpetual Concern

Discorides, the Ancient Greek scientist and philosopher, provided the first description of how rose oil was made. The rose's tannic and gallic acid contents give it astringent and healing qualities, hence the numerous remedies and beauty products that have been made from it in the form of poultices of petals, lotions of rose water, rose oil, and rose ointments and creams. Until the 19th century, Persia retained a monopoly in the production of rose oil and rose water. Even further back, the Sumerians used to rub their bodies with preparations based on roses.

Roses for Massages

In the time of Ramses III, the Egyptian nobles had themselves massaged by a slave, who probably rubbed their bodies with a rose cream made from extracts of rose petals and andropogon oil. These creams were kept in boxes made of scented wood and ivory, and carved with birds and flowers.

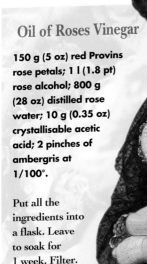

Oil of Roses Vinegar

150 g (5 oz) red Provins rose petals; 1 l (1.8 pt) rose alcohol; 800 g (28 oz) distilled rose water; 10 g (0.35 oz) crystallisable acetic acid; 2 pinches of ambergris at 1/100°.

Put all the ingredients into a flask. Leave to soak for 1 week. Filter.

Purifying Water

In the Middle East, they imported rose water from Damascus. They used it like water to cleanse their temples and mosques. Aladdin had the walls and floor of the mosque of Omar washed in this way, before dedicating it again to Mohammed, after Jerusalem was taken in 1187. Five hundred camels carried the rose water needed for this task.

Spanish leather

In the Middle Ages, the use of perfumes was widely adopted in the royal courts. The great houses of England had a still room, where women distilled the hydrol from flowers. Queen Elizabeth had a clock clad in Spanish leather, perfumed shoes and a pair of gloves decorated with dyed silk roses. Spanish leather, a chamois leather soaked in various essences (orange blossom, rose, lavender, clove, sandalwood, cinnamon, musk, civet, etc.) recalled the odour of human skin.

Opposite top: Advertisement by Georges Lepape, 1925. Musée International de la Parfumerie, Grasse.

Opposite bottom: Anton Eisle, *Portrait of Elizabeth of Austria* (detail), 1837. Private Collection, Vienna.

Right: Narcisse Virgile Diaz de la Peña, *Wild Girls*, 19th century. Musée du Louvre, Paris.

Below:
Lithograph by Devéria, *Venus at Her Toilet Helped by a Cherub*, 19th century. Coll. Arch. Dép. 94.

Opposite left:
Young Woman with Flowers, Roman mosaic pavement, 4th century. Basilica of Aquileia, Venetia.

The Apothecary's Pots

Ancient Eastern, Asiatic and European writings made much of the virtues of the rose, its hips, leaves and roots, used to make remedies for many illnesses, some with supernatural results.

Treatments and Embalmings

In Greece, in very far-off times, people used oils, in which rose petals were soaking, at religious and embalming ceremonies. Merchants brought ointments to Rome made chiefly from roses; these were made in the countries of

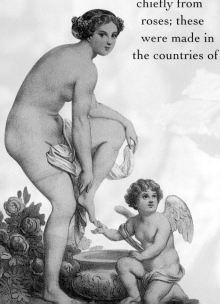

Africa, Syria, Arabia, India and the Far East. In pre-Christian Europe, the dead were burnt on funeral pyres made of eglantine wood.

What Rose Petals Are Made Of

Rose petals consist of oily substances, essential oil, gallic acid, albumin, tannin, colouring matter, salts based on potassium and lime, silica and iron oxide.

The hips of the eglantine contain a significant quantity of vitamin C, iron, phosphorus and vitamins B, E and K.

Popular Medicine

Rose powder cures fluxes: haemorrhages, haemoptysis, diarrhoea, leucorrhea. Its syrup softens the voice. It dissolves kidney stones (gravel), disinfects and cures bites by rabid dogs. Rose syrup and rose water help people to sleep (India). Preserves of red roses treat chronic coughs and colic sweats. The powder of rose petals fortifies the stomach and helps the digestion. The roots of *Rosa rugosa* have a medicinal use in

They have a role in curing wounds and in the production of adrenalin. Infusions of rosehips are tonic, astringent, carminative and diuretic.

THE LEAVES

In herbal medicine, eglantine buds are prescribed to stimulate the secretion of glucocorticoid hormones (cortisol) by the adrenal gland. Infused leaves are applied to wounds in the form of a poultice.

China. The seeds, or achenes, of the rose plant treat gout, oedemas, rheumatism and sciatica. The rosehips, eaten raw, expel worms.

Today's Remedies

ROSEHIPS
Infusions of eglantine hips help to fight flu; it is recommended for fevers, chills, infections and tiredness (often taken as a rosehip tea). The hips also stimulate the appetite and strengthen immunity.

Rose Water, Oil and Essence

Rose water is a skin cleanser. The essential oil is recommended for treating wrinkles, and regenerating tissues and cells. Used with lavender, rose essence may help to treat cancer: 1 drop of

Treatise on Rhodology by Johann Karl Rosenberg, 1628. Coll. Arch. Dép. 94.

Below:
Earthenware pharmacy pot. Coll. Arch. Dép. 94.

essential oil diluted in 100 drops of lavender oil, taken five times a day. The essence of Amazon rose is used by surgeons for healing wounds.

The World of Perfume

Recognising a floral scent, particularly a rose's, is a very personal matter. It just needs the surrounding air to contain the scent of leaves, straw, grass or hay, or to be damper or drier ... and everything changes.

In the same way, when a perfumer creates a perfume and chooses his floral scents, that perfume will also be influenced by the wearer's skin odour and personality.

A Phantom from a Rose

In the 1950s, the chemist Henri Deveaux managed to make the 'phantom' of scents materialise. He spread a thin layer of talc on the surface of a tank of mercury. Then, holding a thread bearing a solid fragment taken from a highly scented rose, he brought this close to the surface he had prepared. The talc parted and a grey stain formed, spreading over the clean surface of the metal. In ten minutes, seven rose petals, placed over the talc-covered mercury, exposed an area of 170 cm² (26 sq in). This phenomenon was photographed.

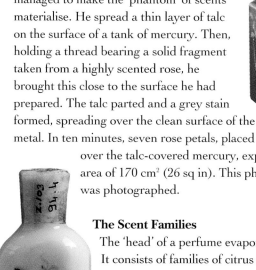

The Scent Families

The 'head' of a perfume evaporates first. It consists of families of citrus fruits (lemon, mandarin, bergamot) and herbs (aniseed, lavender, citronella, basil); it constitutes the 'spirit' and freshness of the perfume. The heart of the perfume, its 'personality', comes from families of flowers (rose, jasmine, lilac, carnation, lily of the valley), fruits (raspberry, pear, peach, apple, apricot), greenery (grass, ivy, leaves) and spices (clove, nutmeg, cinnamon, pepper, ginger). The base, or perfumed 'vapour' of a rose perfume, is made from woody (sandalwood, cedar, patchouli, moss, vetiver) and balsamic elements (vanilla, heliotrope, tonka beans).

Right:
For Cacherel's
Eau d'Eden,
Jean-Paul
Goude created
this marvellous
'skin of roses'
worn by Estella
Warren,
photographed in
an allegorical
scene by its
creator.

Opposite top:
Porcelain flask
for toilet water.
Coll. Arch.
Dép. 94.

**Opposite
far left:**
Glass flask with
polychrome
decoration for
true Eau de
Cologne de
Rosine, created
by Paul Poiret
in 1920. Musée
International de
la Parfumerie,
Grasse.

**Opposite
bottom:**
Opaline glass
flask from
Germany, 18th
century. Musée
International de
la Parfumerie,
Grasse.

'William Shakespeare'® rose *ausroyal*
Delbard.

Below:
A fan of notes for a rose perfume.

A Festival of Scents for a Perfume

A rose perfume is made up of scented notes from various families: hesperidic, floral, fern, chypre, woody, amber and leather. Each family releases its own evocations, which provide markers for creators of perfumes and perfumers.

The Thoughts of a Creator of Rose Perfumes

When he was very young, his head full of dreams, Jean-François Laporte discovered the walled gardens of Grenada with their combination of overpowering sunshine and cooling shade.
The shady area was full of the scents of spices, musk, cinnamon, ripe figs, almonds, pomegranates and jasmine. He was overcome by their perfumes, fierce, heavy and silky like the raucous cries of flamenco. In this town ruled by love,

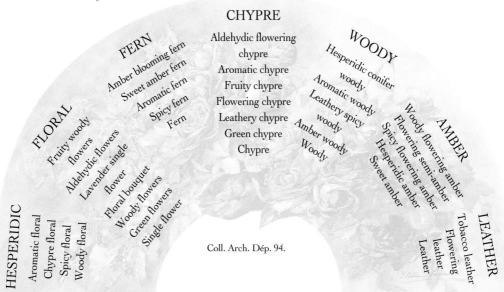

CHYPRE

FERN

WOODY

Aldehydic flowering chypre
Aromatic chypre
Fruity chypre
Flowering chypre
Leathery chypre
Green chypre
Chypre

Amber blooming fern
Sweet amber fern
Aromatic fern
Spicy fern
Fern

Hesperidic conifer woody
Aromatic woody
Leathery spicy woody
Amber woody
Woody

FLORAL

Fruity woody flowers
Aldehydic flowers
Lavender single flower
Floral bouquet
Woody flowers
Green flowers
Single flower

AMBER

Woody flowering amber
Flowering semi-amber
Spicy flowering amber
Hesperidic amber
Sweet amber

HESPERIDIC

Aromatic floral
Chypre floral
Spicy floral
Woody floral

LEATHER

Tobacco leather
Flowering leather
Leather

Coll. Arch. Dép. 94.

he met a passionate young woman who grew roses with delicious scents, in particular a yellow rose with an intoxicating perfume. This encounter made him decide to become a creator of perfumes.

The episode shows how strong images and intense memories combine to feed the imagination of perfumers.

According to Jean-François Laporte, rose and jasmine are the main forces in the creation of perfumes; the perfumer's quest to acquire the countless scents of flowers never ends.

For him, the rose is an inexhaustible source of sensations associated with fragility, delicacy, sensual beauty and gentleness.

It is the pretext for amorous conversations, for refined emotions. Jean-François Laporte, a master perfumer and glovemaker, then created his 'Rose Opulente'.

Famous Rose Perfumes

- **Rose, by Molinard, created in 1860.**
- **Rose Jacqueminot, by Coty, created in 1904.**
- **La Rose d'Orsay, created in 1908.**
- **Rose is Rose, by Houbigant, created in 1974.**
- **Tea Rose, by Perfumer's Workshop, created in 1976.**
- **Trésor, by Lancôme, created in 1990; the famous house launched a perfume 'd'or rose', in which the notes of rose prevail.**
- **Rose Opulente, by Jean-François Laporte, 1990.**
- **Eau d'Eden, by Cacharel, 1996.**

Top left:
'Citron Fraise'® roses *delcifra* Delbard.

Left:
'Impératrice Farah'® rose *delivour* Delbard.

Above:
'Mitsouko'® rose *delnat* Delbard.

Far left:
Opaline glass flask from Germany, end 18th century. Musée International de la Parfumerie, Grasse.

Growing Roses for Perfume

Rose perfumes are everywhere in these fields of the gods. In Ancient times, people in many countries thought that growing roses was one of the greatest riches of their homeland. Today, the growers are as busy as ever supplying the perfume industry and others which also use rose extracts for their products, particularly in Morocco and the countries of eastern Europe.

The Valley of Roses

Ever since the invasion of the Balkan peninsula by the Turks around 1500, damask roses have been grown between two mountain chains, on the heights of Sredna Gora and near the towns of Klissoura, Stara-Planina and Kazanlak in Bulgaria, where the famous 'Valley of Roses' is to be found.

Grasse, City of Flowers and Perfumes

Several species of rose were grown to make perfume in Grasse and its near-neighbours Italy and Morocco: *Rosa centifolia*, introduced to France at the end of the 16th century, which yields a unique product; and the May rose, a hybrid of the Provins rose (*Rosa gallica*), which was brought back from the Crusades. At present they grow 'Hunier' and 'Rose d'Auribeau', spineless varieties of *R. centifolia* (Provence hybrids).

The Valley of Dadès in Morocco

In the valley of Dadès and on the sides of Mont M'goun, on the southern slopes of the Atlas range, they grow *Rosa damascena*. To begin with, the rose bushes were grown by smallholders in dense hedges enclosing the arable fields. In 1937, rose growing in Dadès became

Field of roses at sunset in Gulistan, land of roses, Isparta, Turkey.

industrialised. The buds of dried roses were used to produce a second-grade rose water for confectionery, patisseries, condiments and remedies. The valley of Dadès is located at an altitude of about 1,300 metres (4,260 ft); it is broad and green, watered by streams from the snowy slopes of the Atlas which the feed the wadi of Dadès.

Rose Growing Throughout the World

Roses were, and still are, grown in other countries, each of which has favoured a particular variety.

Thus, in Egypt, we know that *Rosa × richardii* (formerly known as *Rosa sancta* was grown. Today they grow *Rosa gallica* there. In Turkey, Pakistan, India (Punjab and Uttar Pradesh) and in the region of Tbilisi in Georgia, they grow large quantities of *Rosa damascena*. In Japan, *Rosa rugosa* 'Thund' is the most widespread variety.

Opposite top:
The valley of Dadès, Morocco.

Top:
Damask rose.

Left:
Worker picking roses for perfume at Isparta, Turkey.

Background:
R. Hempel, *Harvesting Roses in Bulgaria*, wood engraving by Katzler. Coll. Arch. Dép. 94.

Famous Scented Roses

- Floral bouquet: 'Lavender Dream', 'Impératrice Farah'.
- Geranium and bergamot: 'Rio Ressence'.
- Geranium, citronella, violet: 'Mamy Blue'.
- Geranium, citronella, rose: 'Sharifa Asma'.
- Clove and cinnamon: 'Apogée', 'Blush Damasc'.
- Sweet pea: 'Vanity'.
- Rose and vanilla: 'Léonie Lamecsh'.
- Carnation, clove, vanilla: 'Château de la Juvenie', 'Imbricata', 'Paul Gauguin'.
- Rose: *R. centifolia*, damask rose, Portland rose, *R. rugosa*.
- Aniseed, violet, narcissus: 'The Pilgrim'.
- Citronella, orange, orange blossom, grass, apricot: 'Tobago'.
- Grapefruit, pear, rose: 'William Shakespeare'.
- Grass, violet, raspberry: 'Mitsouko'.
- Citronella, musk, moss, narcissus: 'Nil Bleu'.
- Orange blossom, fennel, cyclamen, fern, patchouli, mushrooms: 'Graham Thomas'.

Flower of Passion

Roses play a part in all the precious moments that life has to offer. They have always inspired the dormant poet in us. Artists and craftsmen choose the rose for what it suggests with its beauty and its symbols. Hostesses use them to brighten up their party tables, and women of taste like to have embroidered, engraved or painted roses on their dressing tables. Food lovers like them too, and there are those who cannot eat well without having the flavours of rose on their tongue. Roses enable us to make a work of art out of every moment in life.

An Inspiration for Craftsmen

The rose has a special place in the decorative arts. We find it reproduced in the form of seedlings, bouquets, friezes and crowns. In both stylised and realist forms, it has been used for tapestries, then for the first wallpapers, from the 15th century to our own time. It is painted on porcelain, engraved on glass and silver, and printed on cloth.

Binding sample by the gilder Ledeux, gilded with leaves and a mosaic pattern. Coll. Arch. Dép. 94.

Previous pages: J.A. Laurent, *To Beauty*. Coll. Arch. Dép. 94.

Rose Sculptures

Roses modelled in glass originally came from Germany and the city of Prague, capital of crystal. In 1740, the Vincennes factory in France produced an original line in flowers of white and polychrome porcelain. The rose and the lily were the favourite models. The flowers were modelled by hand, petal by petal for the rose, then mounted on a metal stem, dried and fired.

These flowers were made into bouquets of different sizes and heights. There are mentions of bouquets of more than a hundred flowers, presented in vases of white porcelain mounted on bronze pedestals.

Roses Painted on Porcelain

Madame de Pompadour imposed her taste on the French court, and it became the taste of the age. Chinese porcelain characterised this style, winning prominence thanks to its floral motifs: seedlings, bouquets, friezes, crowns and garlands decorated the dishes, bowls, plates, cups, teapots and cafetières. The Royal Manufactory of Sèvres produced the most famous tea and dinner services. After the 18th century, all styles were inspired by the rose.

Painted and Printed Motifs

Embroidered roses, roses painted on leather, printed on cotton, silk and lace – these exceptional pieces from public and private collections show the extraordinary inspiration that this flower aroused among artists and craftsmen.

Roses and the Table

Roses bloomed everywhere on cloths and items designed for the table: vases, china, linen and table accessories, lampshades, inlays in furniture, rose-scented pot-pourris, fragrant essences for the household, bouquets, flower arrangements, etc. Although roses now appear more than ever as an ornamental motif around the house, the fact that they are reproduced never seems to impair their freshness.

Porcelain pot with lid. Coll. Arch. Dép. 94.

Below: Sweet box with engraving under glass. Coll. Arch. Dép. 94.

Sub Rosa

In Ancient Rome, the walls of rooms were painted with mythological and floral motifs. When a rose was hung in a room where guests gathered, they knew they must not give away what was said or confided, hence the expression _sub rosa_, literally 'under the rose'.

Left: Games box. Coll. Arch. Dép. 94.

Opposite top: Pot-pourri. Strasbourg Manufactory, c. 1758. Musée National de la Céramique, Sèvres.

Opposite background: Blue plate with rose motif, made at the Van der Does factory, Delft. Musée National de la Céramique, Sèvres.

Background centre: Fantasy bracelet. Coll. Arch. Dép. 94.

An Inspiration for Fashion Designers

There are roses painted on the leather of fashion accessories, embroidered and woven in silk, tulle, velvet, brocade ... engraved and carved in the ivory, mother-of-pearl, gold and silver of jewellery. Pearl roses adorn evening gowns, hairstyles and hats, court shoes...

Embroidered and Artificial Roses

In Egypt they developed the art of wearing fresh roses in spring. Faded roses had to be 'reinvented'. Then they made rings and crowns of roses with strips of horn, material, paper, and dyed wood shavings. These artificial roses were perfumed with oil or cream of rose. In Europe women wore – and since the 16th century continue to wear – silk or lace roses, some sprinkled with sequins in cloudy and rainbow colours. They were made with silk ribbons in various colours, knotted together and fixed on a rigid stem.

A Privilege for Rose Pickers

Under Louis XI, the makers of floral hats were authorised to pick roses for decorating hats on Sundays, the day when all manual work was forbidden. These 'rose hats' were very fashionable at the time. On special occasions, they were the only 'finery' worn by the young damsels.

Pearl Roses on Handbags

In England, at the end of the 16th century and the beginning of the 17th, all garments were decorated with cuffs, belts, ruffs and embroidered collars. Bustiers, gloves and shoes were encrusted with pearls. This was

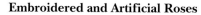

an age famous for the discoveries of travelling botanists, and craftsmen found inspiration in botanical works and illuminated manuscripts.

The Accessory of Elegant Women

At the end of the 19th century, artificial flowers were in fashion. Many popular magazines appeared in English and French, revealing the secrets of how to make them. For roses, there was a pattern which had seven variants enabling people to make roses with different numbers of petals. Roses used as models included the eglantine, the May rose, the pompom rose, the Provence rose and the Bengal rose.

Silk Roses

Today, silk or cloth roses are used by the great couturiers, and sold in certain stores with fashion accessories. They are made by a small number of highly specialised craft workers, whose profession is tending to die out. Other craft workers produce artificial flowers, including roses. You can find these in shops in the accessories department.

Opposite far left: Dress with star-shaped roses, designed by Kenzo, spring/summer 1994 collection.

Opposite left: Rose hat, contemporary design by Marie Mercié.

Opposite top: Back of embroidered waistcoat, haute couture by Christian Lacroix, summer 1990 collection.

Background: Fashion engraving (detail), 19th century. Coll. Arch. Dép. 94.

Left and below: *Jules et Jim*, haute couture by Louis Féraud, spring/summer 1996 collection. Here Louis Féraud follows a traditional line of inspiration for the famous fashion house, based on flowers.

Dufy, Painter of Roses and the Joy of Living

Before flowers became stylised by the Art Deco movement, the painter Raoul Dufy met the couturier Paul Poiret and illustrated cards, letterheads, labels and invitations for the famous fashion house. Their friendship and mutual sympathy led to the creation of new cloths printed with roses and red peonies using the process of wood engraving. Later, Dufy worked for a long time with the Bianchini-Férier company, which he supplied with many sketches often featuring roses, either singly or in a bouquet.

The Painters' Favourite Model

Over the years, many paintings, songs and literary works have described the virginity of Mary, the bird in love with a rose, the muses, gods and goddesses, heroes, queens, empresses, pretty women and fresh young girls. All were adorned with roses.

The Virgin and Her Model in the Middle Ages

Although the rose did not really inspire the primitive, Italian and Flemish masters, it did become the symbolic motif associated with the Virgin Mary. It appears in the walled and secret gardens of the medieval lords, along with the white lily.

Portraits of Roses in the 17th Century

In the 17th century, the rose became a favourite subject of Flemish painters (Brueghel, Bosschaert, Van Aelst and Van Walscapelle among others), sensitive to the beauty of old-fashioned roses and their subtle colouring. Many canvases with the title 'Painting with Flowers' were commissioned by rich merchants and collectors who adored all botanical themes. Since then the rose has appeared constantly in paintings.

Elisabeth Louise Vigée-Lebrun, portrait of Queen Marie-Antoinette known as the *Portrait with Rose* (detail). Musée National du Château et de Trianon, Versailles.

Watercolour

Watercolour is the most subtle pictorial technique for capturing the delicacy and vivacity of the rose's various colours.

Opposite top:
A. Chaplin, *Rose and Convolvulus Resting on a Wall.* Coll. Arch. Dép. 94.

Right:
Vincent Van Gogh, *Roses and Anemones*, 1890. Musée d'Orsay, Paris.

Below:
Fan with red roses painted by Stella Samson. Coll. Arch. Dép. 94.

The Rose and the Souls

The tomb said to the rose:
'Flowers, you are watered by
the dawn
What do you do, flower of love?'

The rose said to the tomb:
'What do you do
with all that falls
Into your ever-open chasm?'

The rose said:
'Dark tomb
With these flowers
I make a perfume of
amber and honey
in the shade.'

The tomb said:
'Plaintive flower,
For every soul
that comes to me
I make an angel
in heaven!'

Victor Hugo
Les Voix Intérieures
(extract), 1880.

Lami, *The Silence of the Tomb*, presented at the Salon de la Sculpture in Paris in 1905. Coll. Arch. Dép. 94.

Mysterious Fans

The fan opens with a rapid movement to reveal its mysterious illustrations, often alluding to love, delighting the eyes of anyone standing near. It is a synonym for elegance and romance. Fans came from Korea and China, and were made of paper or cloth, tortoiseshell, mother-of-pearl and scented sandalwood, and were often decorated by great artists. Pissarro painted 27 of them, and he is not alone: Gustave Moreau, Gauguin, Degas, Caillebotte, Berthe Morisot and Maurice Denis all rose to the pictorial challenge of the fan's semi-circle. An exhibition showing 42 artists' fans was held at the Salon des Beaux-Arts in Paris in 1870. Mallarmé gave fans to his friends after he had personalised them with a poem.

Roses for Special Occasions

Who has not chosen a rose as an accessory to celebrate St Valentine's Day, a birthday or a marriage, or to mark a sad moment? All the special occasions in life seem to feature roses and the things they inspire: bouquets, crowns, garlands and baskets of roses, hearts of roses, postcards, boxes, handkerchieves, embroidered napkins, pot-pourris, perfumed sachets, scented candles, perfumes, spring dresses, etc.

angels and bouquets of roses. In the 19th century, people could talk with flowers. Messages, envelopes and stamps show this.

Where Do Babies Come From?

Little girls are born in the petals of a faded rose, and not in cabbages! The allegory linking the rose and the female sex could not be clearer.

St Catherine's Day

St Catherine and her *catherinettes*, girls aged 25 and still unmarried, hearts to be taken, surprised, loved; they too can be won by roses!

Much Love From...

Love hovers and flies away... The heart in love has wings,

The Delights of Marriage

A large white bed, a white bed covered with rose petals ...

a romantic dream, the idea of roses being always present at the erotic moments in our lives.

Golden Weddings

People live a long time in Europe, which means lots of silver and golden weddings. So much the better! Like Demeter, goddess of Earth and Summer, let us pick the golden flowers and fruits in autumn. She goes to sanction the marriage of

Persephone, wife of Hades in the underworld. When the dormant seeds germinate, it is a sign of Nature's rebirth. The goddess of Spring will come as soon as the severe cold period ends.

Superstitions

They say that God's work created man and the rose, and that of the devil beauty and the eglantine, the 'witch rose'.
They say that when rose petals fall to the ground, they bring bad luck.
They say (but who knows?): 'If you hold a rose in your hand and all its petals fall to earth, it is a sign of bad luck. An omen of death!'

The rose motif has inspired many postcards and wedding announcements. Coll. Arch. Dép. 94.

Roses for Flower Arrangers

To the Ancient Japanese, everything in nature was perfect. The art of flowers was a religion and a moral doctrine. It is through our ignorance of this philosophy that we have relegated them to ornamentation. In Japan, they founded the first schools of flower arranging, and that was in the 8th century according to Dutch travellers and old Japanese manuscripts.

Top:
'Léonidas' var. *meicofum* rose. It has a caramel colour and is famous for the delicate beige tint on the edge of its petals that makes it so elegant.

Right:
Bouquet and crown for Ava, a modern young bride.

The Art of Flowers in Europe Today

A real effort has been made in Europe to educate young florists and arrangers. It is a recognised craft. Schools, educational studies, professional courses and international flower-arranging competitions open new professional and creative possibilities for young flower lovers. But do they teach them that flowers are the glorification of beauty and the harmony of nature, and not of oneself? Roses are used singly or placed with other flowers, helping to make up magnificent bouquets, sprays and crowns for every occasion in life.

One, Three, Six or Twelve?

It is up to the florist to decide how many roses to use. Some roses have a fairly upright stem, and the buds and flowers are well formed; these will be sold singly or used in the heart of a classic bouquet. Only the colour, rather than the number, is symbolic and determines the choice of flowers. We also find so-called garden roses with a more flexible bearing and marvellous colours. Finally, there are the branching roses such as 'Evelyne' and 'Nikita', whose stems are decorated with clusters of small flowers. All these are modern roses grown

Garden of Mustard Seed, Chinese print, 18th century. Musée des Arts Asiatiques Guimet, Paris. Inscription: 'Red flowers separate the leaves, the branches turn, the colour is pale. When you pick them, beware of the compact spines, eat slowly, enjoy their scent.'

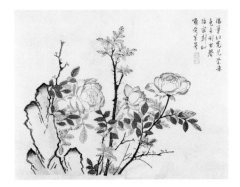

industrially in Morocco, Israel, Kenya and Peru. There are very few European producers, who see their trade being cut back by this international competition.

The names of roses reflect countries, film stars, political figures, famous artists ... and all fashionable people. 'Baccara': a rose with red flowers, created by Meilland and flowering in summer. This has been the best-selling rose in recent years, but it is tending to disappear from the market. 'Jacaranda': slightly blue flowers. 'Pavarotti', 'Ravel': flowers with fuchsia tones. 'Marilyn', 'Vivaldi': pale-pink flowers. 'First', 'Red Rouge', 'Gala': strong red flowers. 'Frisco', 'Texas': flowers with yellow tones. 'Bianca', 'Message': white roses. 'Aznavour', 'Jean Marais', 'Léonie Campbell', 'Charles de Gaulle': flowers with delicious scents.

Bottom:
Bouquet of roses in a blue vase.

Background:
Artist unknown, *Yellow and Blue Vase with Roses*. Coll. Arch. Dép. 94.

The Soul of Flowers

The emperor Henrensung had musicians go with him in spring to delight the flowers with sweet sounds.

The beautiful Somedono arranged branches of flowering cherry before receiving her husband.

In the Tang and Song dynasties, a monk-gardener was appointed to each flower, and instructed to look after it and wash its leaves with a fine brush of rabbit fur.

Roses in the House

A bouquet of old-fashioned roses on the table, another with a runner decorated with white roses, garlands of roses to celebrate the month of May, a party menu, scented bowls, a pot-pourri... It just needs a little imagination and a few basic materials: glue, metal wire, dried flower petals, spices and scented leaves.

A Romantic Bouquet

Choose old-fashioned roses with a rich, full shape in a mixture of colours. Take a vase with a wide opening and fill it with water. Trim the stems, bearing in mind that the flowers at the heart of the bouquet should be a little taller. Arrange the flowers in a ball shape, just leaning over the sides if it suits them. Alternatively, you can make a stylish display by adding ivy or other foliage.

Right:
Drying roses in Morocco.

Top:
Bouquet of pale roses.

Opposite:
Garland of roses and pot-pourri.

Background:
Crown of embroidered flowers. Coll. Arch. Dép. 94.

A Garland of Fresh Roses with Mimosa

In spring, use fresh fuchsia-coloured roses and mimosa to make a magnificent garland. Insert the stems of the flowers inside a plait of ivy. Don't hesitate to mix roses with green elements (moss, leaves and fruit) and with other dried objects such as pine cones. If you use small limes, pierce them right through with a sharp point, slide a metal wire inside and use this to attach them. Fix everything else with plastic-coated wire.

Drying Roses

People used to bury roses in sand which was kept warm until the flowers were completely dehydrated. Once houses became well heated, flowers could be dried in dust under glass globes. You can make dried roses by tying them in tight bunches that are then hung up for a fortnight in a dark, dry, warm, sheltered place. You can also dry them in the microwave oven, which is suitable for flowers only: just keep a small length of stem, lay

the flowers on the oven tray and heat them for 1 minute at a gentle temperature; inspect them and, if necessary, continue checking them at ten seconds intervals until ready.

A Garland of Dried Roses

Plait some green branches of ivy in a crown (or a long strip). You can strengthen the plait with metal wire of the same length. Slide bunches of ivy between the stems then, with the help of some wire and a glue gun, fix on various decorative elements: moss, leaves, fruit, pine cones, dried roses, etc. Don't hesitate to apply the glue in small mounds so that everything adheres properly. These garlands look pretty on doors, tables and walls.

Pot-pourri of Roses and Spices

Use dried rose leaves and petals in different colours, the dried peel of a lime, cut into small pieces, some dried rosehips, dried mint leaves, 20 cloves, 1 teaspoon of cinnamon powder, small shavings of liquorice root (which you can colour), and natural rose essence.

Mix all the dried ingredients together and intensify the rose scent with a few drops of rose essence.

You can buy dried petals and flowers in Chinese food shops and supermarkets, which you can colour and add scent to. For a note of blue, add dried cornflowers, lavender flowers or delphinium flowers. You can also add powdered iris, which works as a fixative (this can be found at herbalists or pharmacies).

A Menu of Roses

◆

ROSE ROYAL

◆

CHLODNIK AMOROSO

◆

STUFFED PHEASANT WITH
AUTUMN ROSES

◆

HEART OF JOSÉPHINE

◆

ARABICA COFFEE WITH
ROSE PETALS

◆

APHRODITE LIQUEUR

A Bouquet of Flavours

My research into rose flavours, involving 87 fragrant roses, 25 rosehips and two types of foliage, has enabled me to design many recipes using roses. The flavours range from fruity to peppery, musky, floral, woody, lemony, ambers and spices, and are delicious for cooking. For a long time there have been items of confectionery, syrups, jellies and jams made with roses. The Tunisian ras al-hanout is a mixed spice containing dried and powdered rose petals. Today, now that rosebuds with culinary flavours, rose syrups and rose liqueurs are available, you can cook with roses all through the year.

Rose Royal

1 bottle Champagne (Brut de Grand Cru), rose syrup, rose liqueur

• Mix 1 teaspoon of rose liqueur with 4 dessertspoons of rose syrup.
• Pour 1 teaspoon of this mixture into the base of each Champagne flute.
• Open the bottle of Champagne and fill the flutes, then decorate each one with a fresh rose petal.

Chlodnik Amoroso

2 teaspoons dried and ground rosebuds, or 3 fresh fragrant roses (preferably with a fruity or peppery flavour), 10 spinach leaves, 1 small bunch tarragon, 2 parsley sprigs, 2 mint leaves, 1 cucumber, 1 fennel, 1 courgette, 1 white onion, 2 eggs, 30 g (1 oz) butter, 125 g (4 oz) pink shrimps, cooked and shelled, 1 lime, squeezed, 1 glass port, 100g (3.5 oz) crème fraîche, some fresh rose petals to decorate, salt, green pepper

• Carefully wash the spinach and herbs. Peel the cucumber, fennel, courgette and onion. Cut the cucumber into rounds, dice the fennel and the onion. Chop the herbs and mix them with rose petals (chopped beforehand if you use fresh petals).
• Boil the eggs for 10 minutes in boiling water, then cool them under running water and remove the shells. Separate the whites from the yolks and mash separately with a fork. Set aside.
• Melt the butter in a large casserole, then gently brown the cucumber, courgette, fennel and spinach leaves. Add the shrimps, the eggs and the chopped herbs, and pour on 1 litre (1.75 pt) water. Add salt and pepper and leave to cook for about 12 minutes.
• Remove from the heat, add the lime juice, the port and the crème fraîche. Before serving, decorate the surface with rose petals, chopped or whole.

This dish is eaten cold in summer. It takes its name from the Czech word *chlodnik*, which means 'refreshment'. These cold soups can be made in various ways, using vegetables and spices in season.

Delicious Roses

There are many food products made with roses. The craftsmen of the town of Provins, which as early as the 15th century produced rose-based medicines, today make a rose liqueur and rose-flavoured sweets, biscuits, jam and honey. In Paris, you can find culinary rose essence and rose syrup in the Indian groceries. In Tunisia, Morocco and India, they make delicious rose syrups. You can find rose jams and jellies in Poland and Romania.

Confiture à la Rose de Provins

R.Pfister Provins

« Emui moult choses Thibault apporta la Rose. »

Stuffed Pheasant with Autumn Roses

1 good pheasant, 1 bottle Jurançon wine, 200 g (7 oz) chanterelles, 4 lovely fragrant autumn roses for the stuffing, or in winter use rose flavouring if you cannot find fragrant roses, 250 g (9 oz) rosehips, 200 g (7 oz) foie gras (duck), 1 small glass fine champagne, 1 egg yolk, butter, 2 slices smoked bacon, 1 long and thick slice country bread, 1 kg (2.2 lb) Brussels sprouts, salt, black pepper

• Ask your butcher to clean out the pheasant. Clean the inside of the pheasant well and brush with a little wine.

• Wash the chanterelles. Chop half the chanterelles, the rose petals (keeping back 20 to decorate), 2 dessertspoons of rosehips, the foie gras and the pheasant's gizzard. Prepare a stuffing with this chopped mixture and half the fine champagne, then add the egg yolk.

• Stuff the pheasant, brown it and glaze it with a little butter, then place it on a dish, sprinkle on the fine champagne and flambé it. Place the slices of bacon in the bottom of a casserole, cover them with the slice of bread and place the pheasant on top. Spread the rest of the rosehips around it. Add a glass of wine and a little water, add salt and pepper and cook for about 1 hour 15 minutes, adding a little wine from time to time.

• Clean the Brussels sprouts. Steam them for 8 minutes. Salt lightly. Select 20 good sprouts and place each on a rose petal to decorate.

• Brown the rest of the chanterelles in a pan with a little butter. Add salt and pepper.

• Serve the pheasant cut in four with the stuffing at the centre, surrounded by chanterelles and the sprouts on the rose petals. Serve the rest of the sprouts in a dish.

Heart of Joséphine

1 shortcrust pastry, honey or rose jam, rose sugar (see below), 1 l (1.75 pt) full cream milk, 1 vanilla pod, rose syrup, 80 g (3 oz) caster sugar, 3 eggs, 25 g (1 oz) flour, 60 g (2 oz) icing sugar, 20 balls choux pastry (from your delicatessen), 1 rose covered with meringue (see below), crystallised petals (see below under 'Meringue Rose')

• Preheat your oven to 200°C (400°F), gas mark 6–7. Line a pie dish with the shortcrust pastry, leaving the edges free. Prick the surface with a fork and bake blind for 10 to 12 minutes. Put the tart on a dish, brush the edges with honey and dredge with rose sugar.

• In a large casserole, boil the milk, 5 dessert-spoons of rose syrup, the sugar and the vanilla pod (cut lengthways in two beforehand).

• Meanwhile, break the eggs and separate the whites from the yolks. Mix the yolks with 6 dessertspoons of rose syrup into the flour, strain the hot milk and gently add, then return to the casserole and cook until it thickens. Set aside away from the heat.

• Beat the egg whites until stiff with 1 dessertspoon of rose syrup and the icing sugar, and then incorporate carefully into the cooled

confectioner's custard. Cut the choux pastry balls in two and stuff them with this cream.

• Place the stuffed pastry balls around the edge of the tart (sticking them on with a little honey or jam), and pour the rest of the cream into the centre.

• Dredge with rose sugar and decorate with the meringue rose and the crystallised petals.

Rose Sugar

Mix 150 g (5 oz) granulated sugar with 2 dessertspoons of rose syrup until the sugar takes on a lovely pink colour. Keep it in an airtight jar.

Meringue Rose

Wash and dry a beautiful rose. Cut off the stem about 1 cm (½ in) from the flower so you can hold and move it.
Lightly beat an egg white with a fork and dip the rose in it.
Finish off with a brush so that all parts of the rose are covered. Dredge the rose evenly with caster sugar. Dry in the sun or in an oven at 80°C (160°F), gas mark 1 with the door open. Crystallise rose petals in the same way.

Arabica Coffee with Rose Petals

For 4 cups. The previous evening mix 80 g (3 oz) of ground Arabica coffee with 10 petals from a fragrant rose. Before making the coffee, remove the rose petals. Infuse the coffee with hot spring water and serve it with crystallised rose petals.

Aphrodite Liqueur

Wash the petals of 4 fragrant roses. Drain and mix them with 350 g (12 oz) sugar and place in a lidded receptacle, then cover with plum brandy (about 1 litre/1.75 pt) and add the juice of a lemon. Mix well, close the lid and leave to soak for 2 months. When ready, filter the liqueur and put in bottles.

Appendices

That's All Very Well, But Let's Cultivate Our Garden!

Planting a rose bush is like communing with your ancestors. It is a hardy plant, and the method is more or less the same as it was in the past. Roses like a sunny site and to be well cared for.

Planting Period

You can plant a rose bush any time from October to March. However, the rainy days of autumn are the most suitable for a successful

Artificial fertilisation.

Trimming the roots.

planting. From spring to summer you can find rose bushes in containers. Once planted, they need regular and thorough watering. In winter, the young plants are sold with bare roots, enclosed in polythene to protect them. Avoid planting them in frosty periods.

Choosing a Good Rose Plant

The roots of a plant supplied in a container must be thick and fine, filling the whole of the earth ball, and should not be bunched up or protruding from the container. The stems of bushes with bare roots must be well balanced. If the new shoots are pale and etiolated, this indicates that the plants were pulled up a long time ago and stored in poor conditions.

The Planting Hole

Choose a favourable spot in a good sunny position.

Avoid planting your rose bush in a hole vacated by an old plant you have pulled up, or else put in new soil. The hole should be twice as wide as the container, and about 15 cm (6 in) deeper than the height of the container. Break up the soil at the bottom of the hole and mix in a little rotted manure – not fresh manure, which would burn the roots.

Planting the Rose Bush

Slit the polythene cover on both sides and gently ease out the plant. Place it in the centre of the hole and earth up to the top of the union of the stock and scion, which should be buried about 3 cm (1 in). If you plant in spring, sprinkle the soil with a balanced granulated fertiliser. Cover the soil with leaves, bark or peat to stop it drying out and prevent weed growth. For plants with bare roots, it is a good idea to coat these by dipping them in a mixture of water, soil and cow dung. This will help them to become established after planting.

Regular Tasks

There are five rules to follow to keep your roses healthy:
– Prune dead branches, faded flowers and new suckers at the base of the plant.

Coating the roots.

The Rose-lover's Calendar

• **End February–early March: tidy up the beds, fork in rotted manure or compost, hoe level and prune.**
• **April: begin spraying with fungicide.**
• **May–June: pinch out the stems, breaking off the soft tips of vigorous young shoots with your fingers to encourage flowering and to balance the foliage. Cut out any wild growth and water copiously.**
• **July–August: remove dead flowers. Prune non-perpetual climbing roses after flowering.**
• **October: prepare your beds for future planting.**
• **October–November: protect the plants against frost.**

– Fork in manure in early spring, and add balanced fertiliser in June–July.
– Never feed a rose bush at the end of summer.

Form the mulch into a bowl and water into it.

– Spread mulch around the base of the plant in spring. Pine bark adds acid to the soil; best of all are compost, peat and dried leaves.

Black spot.

– Water regularly and copiously in the evening, for roses send their roots deep into the soil, which needs to be well soaked by the end of watering.

Powdery mildew.

Pests and Diseases
The effects of pests and diseases are fairly easy to spot.
– Black spot: appears at the beginning of summer; the leaves develop rusty spots which turn black and lead to the leaf drying out. Remove affected leaves and spray with fungicide.
– Mildew: whitish grey spots appear on the leaves and quickly spread over the plant. Spray with an appropriate fungicide and burn the affected branches after removal from the plant.
– Aphids (greenfly): they love the tender stems of rose plants and mass together at the top of the shoots once the leaves have fallen off. Generate your own 'army' of ladybirds. They will be very efficient, whether fans of chemical treatments like it or not.Chemicals may also be very efficient but destroy beneficial insects and butterflies.

Insect pests on a bud.

Cutting out shoots.

Pruning Roses
The cut should be made above a bud pointing outwards. Pruning is

Removing old wood.

usually carried out after the frosts in spring.
– Hybrid tea roses: lighten the branches and cut them back by half.
– Bush roses with clusters of flowers: cut back weak and old branches. Shorten

Pruning an old shrub.

the remaining branches to two-thirds. Their height should be about 45 cm (18 in).
– Shrub roses: shorten the main stems by a quarter to half their length. Cut out badly situated, exhausted or diseased

Equipment for treating roses.

branches to maintain a balanced shape.
– Climbing roses: keep the branches forming the framework, cut out shoots that have flowered during the year and shorten stems that flowered the previous summer. Prune side shoots to two or three buds.
– Standard roses: shorten the summer shoots by half.
– Weeping roses: cut back stems, retaining new growth. Shorten the side branches to two buds.

Things to See and Do

Visit rose gardens and rose growers, go to flower shows and exhibitions, and consult specialist books and magazines to improve your knowledge and help you choose varieties to plant yourself. There are also tours that visit well-known rose gardens, or you can make up your own route and do it yourself.
Some rose gardens are open only during the growing season. Check first before going.

Great Rose Gardens

Great Britain and Northern Ireland
• David Austin Roses
Bowling Green Lane, Ablighton, nr Wolverhampton, Staffordshire
WV7 3HB
Fax: 44 01902 515621
• City of Belfast International Rose Garden
Sir Thomas & Lady Dixon Park, Belfast, N Ireland
• Crarae Gardens Charitable Trust
Crarae, Inveraray, Argyll, Scotland
PA32 8YA
Tel: 44 01546 886614
• Hidcote Manor Gardens
nr Chipping Campden, Gloucestershire
GL55 6LR
Tel: 44 01386 438333
• Kew Rose Collection
Royal Botanic Gardens, Kew, Richmond, Surrey
TW9 3AB
Tel: 44 020 8332 5655
• Mannington and Wolterton Gardens

Lord and Lady Walpole, Mannington Hall, Itteringham, Norfolk
Tel: 44 01263 584175
• Mattocks Rose Garden
Nuneham Courtenay, Oxfordshire
OX44 9PY
Tel: 44 08457 585652
• Mottisfont Abbey
Mottisfont, Romsey, Hampshire
Tel: 44 01794 340757
• RHS Garden Harlow Carr
Crag Lane, Harrogate, Yorkshire
Tel: 44 01423 505604
• RHS Garden Wisley
Woking, Surrey GU23 6QB
Tel: 44 01483 224234
• Royal National Rose Society
Chiswell Green, St Albans, Hertfordshire AL2 3NR
Tel: 44 01727 850461
Publishes a members' journal, *The Rose*.

United States

• American Rose Center Gardens
8877 Jefferson Paige Road, off I-20 (Exit 5), Shreveport, Louisiana 71119 8811
Tel: 1 318 938 5402, ext 3011
• Elizabeth Park Rose Gardens
915 Prospect Park, Hartford, Connecticut
CT 06105
Voice mail: 1 860 722 6541

• Inez Parker Memorial Rose Garden
Park Blvd at Plaza de Balboa, San Diego, California 992101
• International Rose Gardens
Pocatello, Idaho ID 83201
Voice mail: 1 208 234 6232
• International Rose Test Garden
Washington Park, 400 SW Kingston, Portland, Oregon OR 97201
• Ladd's Addition Rose Garden
SE16 & Harrison, Portland, Oregon OR 97214
• Mesa Community College Rose Garden
1833 W Southern, Mesa, nr Phoenix, Arizona
Tel: 1 602 461 7407
• Peaceful Habitations Rose Gardens
PO Box 2176, 37 Seewald Road, Boerne, Texas 78212
Tel: 1 830 537 4177
• Peninsula Park Rose Garden
N Ainsworth between Kerby & Albina, Portland, Oregon OR 97217

Europe

Belgium
• Kasteel van Hex
3870 Heks
Tel: 32 01274 49 87
• Jardins Ouverts
Chaussée de Vleurgat, 108
1000 Bruxelles
Tel: 32 02646 97 36
• Kasteel van Aartrijke
Zeeweg, 42 – 8820 Torhout

France

• Bagatelle
Direction des Parcs et des Jardins
Route de Sèvres à Neuilly, Bois de
Boulogne 75016 Paris
Tel: 33 01 45 01 20 50
• Roseraie de L'Haÿ-les-Roses
Parc de la Roseraie,
Rue Albert-Watel
94240 L'Haÿ-les-Roses
Tel: 33 01 47 40 04 04
Publishes the journal of
Les Amis de la Roseraie
du Val-de-Marne
• Roseraie de
Joséphine
Château de Malmaison
15, Avenue du
Château-de-Malmaison
92500 Rueil-Malmaison
Tel: 33 01 41 29 05 55
• Roseraie du Parc Floral
de Paris
Bois de Vincennes
16, Route de la Brasserie
75012 Paris
Tel: 33 01 43 43 92 95
• Roseraie du Parc Floral
de la Source
Avenue du Parc Floral
45702 Orléans Cedex 2
Tel: 33 02 38 49 30 00
• Roseraie Saint-Nicolas
Prairie Saint-Nicolas
71380 Chatenoy-en-Bresse
Tel: 33 03 85 48 17 71

Germany

• Europa-Rosarium
Steinberger Weg, 3
06526 Sangerhausen
Tel: 49 03464 57 25 22
• Rosengarten im
Palmengarten
Siesmayerstrasse, 61

60323 Frankfurt-am-Main
Tel: 49 069 212 333 83
• Rosengarten Zweibrücken
Wildrosengarten an der Fasanerie
Stadtverwaltungamt 60/67
Gymnasiumstr. 5-7
66482 Zweibrücken
• Wallringpark
Parkteil planten und blömen
 Glacis Haussee, 20
  2000 Hamburg 4

Italy
  • Palazzo Patrizi
  Castel Giuliano
   00062 Bracciano-Roma
   Tel: 39 06 9987 063/203
  • Oasi di Ninfa
   Ninfa, 04010 Norma
   Tel: 39 07 73 69 54 04 17

  Switzerland
   • Roseraie du Parc
 de la Grange
 Thonex, 1226
 Geneva
 Tel: 41 022 736 33 49

*Perfume Museums
of the World*

• Annette Green Museum
Fragrance Foundation
145 East 32nd Street,
9th Floor
New York City, NY, USA
• Cotswold Perfumery
Bourton-on-the-Water
Cheltenham,Gloucestershire,
GL54 2BU, England
Tel: 44 01451 820698
• 4711-Museum
An Farina, Unter

Goldschmied 5-7
50667 Cologne, Germany
Tel: 49 0221 294 1709
• Musée des Arômes de
Provence
Bd Mirabeau,
Saint-Remy-de-Provence,
France
Tel: 33 04 90 92 48 70
• Musée Internationale
de la Parfumerie
8 place du Cours
06130 Grasse, France
Tel: 33 04 93 36 80 20
• Musée de la Parfumerie
9 rue Scribe
75009 Paris, France
Tel: 33 01 47 42 93 40
• Musée de la Parfumerie
Galimard
73 rte de Cannes
06130 Grasse, France
Tel: 33 04 93 09 20 00
• Museu del Parfum
Heaven Scent,
Pg de Gràcia 39
08007 Barcelona, Spain
Tel: 34 093 216 01 46
• Musée du Parfum
Fragonard
Usine Historique
20 Bd Fragonard
06130 Grasse, France
Tel: 33 04 93 36 44 65
• Parfummuseum
Hochfelden
Marianne Maag-Riesen
Chäslenstr. 7
8182 Hochfelden,
Switzerland
Tel: 41 01 860 80 08
• Nederlands
Parfummuseum
Bosstraat 2
1731 SE Winkel, Netherlands
Tel: 31 0224 541578

Bibliography

ATTWATER, Donald, *The Penguin Dictionary of Saints*, Penguin Books, Harmondsworth, 2nd edition, 1983.

AUSTIN, David, *Old Roses and English Roses*, Antique Collectors' Club, Woodbridge, Suffolk, 1992.

Brewer's Dictionary of Phrase & Fable, Millennium Edition revised by Adrian Room, Cassell, London, 2000.

CLARKE, Ethne, *Making a Rose Garden*, Grove Weidenfeld, New York, 1991.

CULPEPER, Nicholas, *Culpeper's Complete Herbal* 17th century, reissued W. Foulsham & Co. Ltd, London.

DELBARD, Henri, *Diary of a Rose Lover*, Harry N Abrams, New York, 1996.

DORRA, Mary Tonetti, *Beautiful American Rose Gardens*, Clarkson Potter, New York, 1999.

DRUITT, Liz, *The Organic Rose Garden*, Taylor Publishing, Dallas, 1996.

FISHER, John, *The Companion to Roses*, Penguin Books, Harmondsworth, Middlesex, 1986.

FOUGÈRE, Paule, *Le Livre des Parfums*, Robert Morel éditeur, 1972.

HALL, James, *Hall's Dictionary of Subjects and Symbols in Art*, John Murray, London, 1974.

HARKNESS, Jack, *Roses*, J M Dent and Sons, London, 1978.

HARKNESS, Peter and MOODY, Mary, *The Illustrated Encyclopedia of Roses*, Timber Press, 1993.

HARRIS, Cyril C, *Roses*, Paul Hamlyn, London, 1969.

HERWIG, Rob, *Your Flower Garden*, Mitchell Beazley, London, 1979.

Larousse Encyclopedia of Mythology, Hamlyn Group, London, new edition 1968.

MCHOY, Peter, *The Ultimate Rose Book*, Lorenz Books, London, 1997.

MUSÉE DE LA ROSE, *La Rose dans tous ses Etats*, catalogue of the Musée de la Rose, Créteil, Paris, 1993.

PHILLIPS, Roger and RIX, Martyn, *Roses*, Pan Macmillan, London, 1988.

ROYAL HORTICULTURAL SOCIETY PLANT GUIDES, *Roses*, Dorling Kindersley, London, 1996.

STEEN, Nancy, *The Charm of Old Roses*, Milldale Press, Washington DC, 1987.

URSE, Nanda d', *Roses du Jardin de Hex*, Editions Ianno, Château de Hex, Tilt, Belgium, 1995.

Acknowledgements

We particularly wish to thank:
• M. Michel Germa, president
of the Conseil Général du
Val-de-Marne;
• Nadine Villalobos, official
representative, Chantal Pourrat,
head of promotion, and Didier Petit,
photographer, management of the
Espaces Verts Départementaux du
Val-de-Marne;
• Françoise Bosman, director,
Corinne Hubert, assistant director,
and Yvon Denis, photographer,
Archives Départementales du
Val-de-Marne;
• Nicole Philippe and Jean
Clarence Lambert for reading
the French texts;
• David Tissier, for his advice on the
classification of roses;
• Lyse Fleurs – 9, quai Georges-
Clemenceau – 78380 Bougival –
for their professional advice;
• Ava Hervier-Debidour;
• Raphaële Martin Lambert;
• Bernard Hervier;
• Armen Tokathian;

• Alain Bernard, the House of Iran
in Paris, Daum France, and the
Parfumerie Fragonard in Grasse for
the loan of illustrations;
• the boutique Au Nom de la Rose –
46, Rue du Bac, Paris;
• the florist Au Nom de la Rose –
87, Rue Saint-Antoine, Paris;
• the hat shop Marie Mercié –
23, Rue Saint-Sulpice, Paris;
• the boutique Siècle – 24, Rue du
Bac, Paris, for the loan of objects.

Rose Collections

The Archives Départementales du
Val-de-Marne have two
complementary collections on roses:
the Musée de la Rose, created by
Jules Gravereaux in the Roseraie
de L'Haÿ, and that bequeathed by
a family of nurserymen from Brie,
the Cochets. The two collections
are accessible thanks to a detailed
catalogue set up in 1993, and for the
art historian form a unique collection
on the subject. In order to make
the public and researchers more
aware of its resources, the Archives
Départementales have set up a bank
of on-screen images which can be
printed out on paper; questions can
also be asked about them.

The Collection of the Musée de la Rose

When Jules Gravereaux had
collected all the species of rose in
preservation, classified them and
compiled a bibliography of
rose science, he had the idea
of forming a museum to keep
and show documents and objects
related to roses. The 1906
publication *Le Rose dans les Sciences,
dans les Lettres et dans les Arts* gives a
detailed account of his collection,
which he never ceased to augment.
The collection contains many
different sections: books and
periodicals, documentary records,
paintings, drawings and prints,
objects inspired by roses... It has
been completed with audiovisual
archives donated by the descendants
of Jules Gravereaux.

The Legrand-Cochet Collection

This collection was bequeathed
to the Roseraie de L'Haÿ-les-Roses
in 1986 and transferred to the
Archives Départementales du
Val-de-Marne. It includes a
complete series of the *Journal des
Roses*, created by Charles Cochet,
notes, correspondence and
specialised works, as well as
an edition of *Roses Peintes par
Pierre-Joseph Redouté* of 1829.

Photographic Credits

Key to Abbreviations: t = top; c = centre; b = bottom; bg = background; l = left; r = right; tl = top left; tr = top right; bl = bottom left; bc = bottom centre; br = bottom right.

© AKG Paris: 21 bl, 23 tl, 76, 86 b; © Coll. Arch. Dép. 94–Y. Denis: front cover, 3, 5 tr, 5 bl, 7 tr, 14 l, 18 bl, 21 t, 22 tr, 22 bl, 24 bl, 26 br, 28 bl, 29 t, 29 b, 30 tl, 30 b, 31 bl, 34–35, 34 tl, 34 bc, 34 tr, 36 bl, 39 tr, 39 bg, 40 bg, 40 tl, 40 tr, 42 bl, 42 tr, 43 bg, 43 b, 51 b, 52 b, 54 b, 55 bg, 57 bg, 58 bl, 61 bg, 63 bg, 64–65 bg, 65 l, 68 b, 68 t, 70 bg, 70 b, 70 t, 74, 79 b, 84 bg, 85 tr, 88 b, 89 tr, 89 b, 90 t, 92 b, 95 bg, 96–97, 98–99 bg, 98 b, 99 t, 99 br, 99 bl, 101 bg, 102 t, 102–103, 103 r, 104 tl, 104 bl, 104 r, 104–105, 105 l, 105 br, 105 tr, 106–107 bg, 109 bg, 110–111, 114 b, 120 bl, 124, 125 l, 125 r, 126 tl, 126 bl, 126 r, 127; © Elia Ascheri: 78 b, 79 t; © Pascal Barin: 101 br; © Delbard: 44 bl, 44–45 bg, 46 t, 46 b, 49 b, 54 br, 56 b, 56 tr, 57 bl, 63 r, 92 t, 93 t, 93 b; © Delbard– Ferret: 93 r; © DEVD 94–D. Petit: 56 tl, 58 t, 60 br, 61 c, 62 l, 64 t, 64 br, 65 t, 123 tr; © Yves Duronsoy: 5 tl, 80–81, 83, 84 t, 85 l, 94 t, 95 t, 107 b, 108 b, 108 t, 109 l; © Ph. Estieu: 69 t; © P. Fernandes/AD: 57 c; © J.–P. Gabriel: 77 t; © G.P.L/John Glover: 58 br; © G.P.L/John Miller: 73 bg; © G.P.L/Gary Rogers: endpapers, 6; © G.P.L/Laslo Puskas: 62 tr; © Giraudon: 17 r, 17 l, 18 t, 25, 26 t, 27 b, 87, 89 tl, 98 bg, 103 t; © Bridgeman–Giraudon: 15; © Lauros–Giraudon: 20 r, 51 bl, 98 t; © Lauros–Giraudon – rights reserved: 50 bl; © J.–P. Goude – Estella Warren – Cacherel: 91; © Grasse, Musée International de la Parfumerie: 7 br, 82 t, 85 b, 86 t, 90 l, 90 b, 93 l; © Jacana–Guy Thouvenin: 71; © J.–B. Leroux–Hoa–Qui: 32–33, 69 bl, 69 br; © Musée du Château de Malmaison: 19 b; © Musée du Château de Malmaison–L. Uran: 19 t, 37, 38 tl, 38 b, 39 tl; © MAP–Arnaud Descat: 39 b, 40 b, 54 t, 55 b, 60 bl, 65 r; © MAP–M. Duyck: 122 br; © MAP–N. and P. Mioulane: 38 tr, 41 t, 43 t, 47 bl, 48 b, 50 t, 50 bl, 52 tl, 52 tr, 53, 60 t, 61 l, 120 t, 120 br, 121 b, 122 tl, 122 bl, 122 c, 123 tl, 123 bl, 123 r; © MAP–Noun: 64 bl; © Guy Marineau: 100 t; © Christian Moser: 100 bl; © Doc. Meilland–E. Ulzega: 30 t, 75 t, 104–105 bg, 106 t; © Marie Mercié–Claude Genet: 100 br; © National Trust Photographic Library/Neil Campbell – Charp: 73 b; © National Trust Photographic Library–Andrew Lawson: 73 t; © National Trust Photographic Library–Stephen Robson: 72 t, 74–75 bg; © Nordisk Pressefoto: 45 b; © Coll. Parfumerie Fragonard de Grasse–H. del Olmo: 84 l; © Coll. Parfumerie Fragonard de Grasse–Bernard Touillon: 88 t; © Jean-Pierre Persmann: 5 bl, 12 t, 16 b, 16 t, 23 b, 101 tr, 106 b, 109 t, 112, 113, 115, 116, 117; © The Photo Source: 78 t; © Poulsen Roser ApS: 45 t, 49 t, 77 b; © RMN: 10 b, 13 b, 35, 102 b; © RMN–Arnaudet: 4; © RMN–P. Bernard: 11; © RMN–J.G. Berizzi: 14 tr; © RMN–Gérard Blot: 8–9, 24 t; © RMN–Richard Lambert: 107 t; © RMN–Lewandowski: 10 t, 13 t, 14 b; © RMN–R.–G. Ojeda: 12 bl; © RMN–Jean Schormans: 20 t, 48 bg; © Roseraie d'André Eve, Pithiviers, © J.–B. Leroux–Hoa–Qui: 66–67; © Paul Starosta: cover and back cover, 36 t, 36 br, 41 b, 43 r, 48 t; © Sygma–Diego Goldberg: 31 t; © Arthur Thévenart: 82 b, 94 t, 95 b; © Agence TOP–M. Balston: 47 t; © Agence TOP–Michel Cognan: 27 t; © Agence TOP–Jerry Harpur: 59; © Traverso: 75 b; © Truffaut: 62 br, 63 l.

Editor: Laurence Basset, assisted by Camille de Cacqueray
Designer: Sabine Houplain
Layout: Corinne Pauvert

First published by Editions du Chêne, an imprint of Hachette-Livre
43 Quai de Grenelle, Paris 75905, Cedex 15, France
Under the title *Le Roman des roses*
© 1999, Editions du Chêne – Hachette Livre
All rights reserved

English language translation produced by Translate-A-Book, Oxford

This edition published by Hachette Illustrated UK, Octopus Publishing Group,
2–4 Heron Quays, London E14 4JP
English Translation © 2004, Octopus Publishing Group, London

Printed in Singapore by Tien Wah Press
ISBN: 1-84430-059-5